furniture care:

REVIVING & REPAIRING **surfaces**

furniture care:

REVIVING & REPAIRING surfaces

professional techniques to bring your furniture back to life

WILLIAM COOK
W. J. COOK & SONS
PHOTOGRAPHY BY JOHN FREEMAN

southwater

This edition is published by Southwater

Southwater is an imprint of Anness Publishing Ltd
Hermes House, 88–89 Blackfriars Road, London SE1 8HA
tel. 020 7401 2077; fax 020 7633 9499; www.southwaterbooks.com; info@anness.com

UK agent: The Manning Partnership Ltd, 6 The Old Dairy, Melcombe Road, Bath BA2 3LR;
tel. 01225 478444; fax 01225 478440; sales@manning-partnership.co.uk

UK distributor: Grantham Book Services Ltd, Isaac Newton Way, Alma Park Industrial Estate,
Grantham, Lincs NG31 9SD; tel. 01476 541080; fax 01476 541061; orders@gbs.tbs-ltd.co.uk

North American agent/distributor: National Book Network, 4501 Forbes Boulevard, Suite 200, Lanham,
MD 20706; tel. 301 459 3366; fax 301 429 5746; www.nbnbooks.com

Australian agent/distributor: Pan Macmillan Australia, Level 18, St Martins Tower, 31 Market St, Sydney,
NSW 2000; tel. 1300 135 113; fax 1300 135 103; customer.service@macmillan.com.au

New Zealand agent/distributor: David Bateman Ltd, 30 Tarndale Grove, Off Bush Road, Albany,
Auckland; tel. (09) 415 7664; fax (09) 415 8892

Publisher: **Joanna Lorenz**
Editorial director: **Judith Simons**
Project editors: **Charlotte Berman, Lucy Doncaster and Claire Folkard**
Text editor: **Alison Bolus**
Designer: **Lisa Tai**
Photographer: **John Freeman**
Technical director: **Paul Lyon, W.J. Cook & Sons**
Editorial reader: **Richard McGinlay**
Production controller: **Claire Rae**

Previously published as part of a larger volume, *The Complete Guide to Repairing & Restoring Furniture*

1 3 5 7 9 10 8 6 4 2

PUBLISHER'S NOTE
The author and publisher have made every effort to ensure that all instructions contained in this book are accurate and that
the safest methods are recommended. The publisher and the author cannot accept liability for any resulting injury, damage
or loss to persons or property as a result of using any tools in this book or carrying out any of the techniques or projects.
Before you begin any restoration task, you should know how to use all your tools and equipment safely and be sure and
confident about what you are doing.

CONTENTS

INTRODUCING SURFACE RESTORATION

Whatever the date, period or style, at some point all antique furniture will need its surfaces repaired and restored. In the past, repairs were often simply fashioned to make the piece serviceable, sometimes not even in the timber of the original. But with the burgeoning interest in antiques, what was seen as secondhand furniture is now valued for its character and rarity. Today's restorer and polisher aims to bring out the existing surface patination.

In medieval times the original cabinet-maker or the local estate joiner made repairs. However, in later pieces works have often been carried out that are obviously not by the same hand as the original cabinet-maker. With changing fashions, pieces were adapted to make them more suitable for a particular task. This could range from legs being added, to handles being changed to reflect current styles and pieces being reduced in size. A classsic example is bun feet, fashionable during the late 17th century but often replaced by the new style of bracket feet during the 18th century. The original bun feet absorbed moisture from standing on stone floors laid directly on to earth foundations and rotted away.

Understanding the construction of furniture, including the cabinet-making techniques and the type of finish used during its period, is vital. Equally important is access to the correct tools, a suitable work environment and, when necessary, antique timbers to patch damaged areas. Selecting the correct matching piece of timber can greatly reduce the time spent trying to match a repair to the original surface in the polishing shop. Before beginning any restoration project, possible problems should be analysed and the best solutions realized. Otherwise, the easiest of tasks can soon develop into a major undertaking. It makes no sense to begin polishing a piece of furniture, only to discover that not enough polish or stain is to hand.

Right: *A pair of 18th-century pedestals displaying superb colour and patination, which take generations to develop.*

Often, working on a small test piece or area will help to avoid unforeseen problems. Understanding how styles developed and changed is important, too – for instance, why varnish and wax were used in the 17th century, oil in the 18th and shellac polish at the start of the 19th century. These are all altered by time and develop their own distinctive surfaces. This patination, best described as the history of a piece in its surface, is what can greatly increase an antique's value. With cabinet work, restoration research is needed to know what may have originally been present. As fashions changed, galleries, mouldings and mounts were altered or replaced. The aesthetics of a piece can be rebalanced by the removal and correct replacement of a later addition. Likewise, removing later finishes and applying a more suitable one can bring the character of a piece nearer its original condition.

A huge responsibility rests upon the shoulders of the antique restorer, now often expected to take on the dual roles of cabinet-maker and polisher. In front of him is a piece of history, with a surface that has developed its unique qualities over centuries. This uniqueness can be lost in an instant if the restorer applies the wrong methods. Bad restoration or over-zealous cleaning of a patinated surface by the inexperienced, unqualified or unsupervised is nothing short of criminal. Wherever possible colour and patination should be retained.

The actual mechanics of polishing are dealt with in detail later in the book but, as with restoration versus conservation, there are two schools of thought. Some prefer that nothing other than wax is applied. While this seems logical and is on occasion best, often a piece loses its lustre as the top layers of polish perish. In such cases the layers should be gently removed and replaced to allow the various hues and tones of the timber below to show in their full glory. It is this area that requires the greatest skill as once generations of built-up surface have been stripped away no amount of subsequent waxing will replace them. A balance must be established for the best possible result.

The importance of the restorer is increasing greatly as both the trade and public are buying more antique furniture that requires attention before it can be sold or used. The next generation inheriting furniture are realizing the value of their legacies and appreciating the skill and workmanship involved in the original construction. They know that furniture must be well cared for and properly restored if it is to survive.

Those who are prepared to learn their craft thoroughly while they are building up their historical knowledge, not to mention their supplies of timber, and increasing their practical ability, can be

Above: *As well as colouring and polishing small patches of repair, the polisher must be able to work on much larger areas.*

assured of a rewarding interest or career. As with everything in life, what one puts in is what one takes out – never more so than in the field of antique furniture restoration.

Above: *Even the worst damage, such such as burns, can be restored when the right techniques are employed.*

Left: *One of the most common types of surface damage is a water stain.*

PURCHASING

There are two main sources for buying antique furniture: a dealer (either trade or retail) and an auction room. Antique fairs are another good source, providing a range of competing stalls from which to buy. Lastly, for the internet fan there is on-line buying, which is still in its infancy. All these sources have their advantages and disadvantages, and it is for individual buyers, after careful consideration, to choose their preferred method.

AUCTION ROOMS

Most towns and cities will have their own auction room holding regular sales of antiques. A catalogue describing each lot is provided, and, depending on the auction house and the sale being held, photographs will also often be included as well as pre-sale estimates. Always make sure you read the conditions of sale and the terms of business very carefully. Almost all auction rooms will charge a buyer's premium, with purchase tax being added on to this premium. Be sure to calculate this properly, since it can make a considerable difference between the bid price and the actual invoice figure.

View each lot carefully, making a note of any damage. If you want to make a bid, decide on a figure that you will be comfortable with paying, taking into account any buyer's premium and tax. Most auction rooms will require you to register before you can bid. Having decided on a price, stick to it, as the most common mistake when buying at auction is to enter into a battle with another bidder, secure the lot and then realize that, in your determination to have it, you have paid far more than you had intended. One of the biggest disadvantages of buying at auction is that once you have bid and secured your purchase, you cannot change your mind about buying the piece. Once the auctioneer's hammer has come down, the goods are yours.

Finally, most private individuals feel that by buying at auction they are getting the piece at a cheaper price than buying from a dealer. You may, on occasion, secure a bargain, but since most sales are well subscribed and viewed by dealers, you should remember that, more often than not, there may be a good reason why a dealer has decided not to bid.

Above: *Auction rooms, where both traders and private individuals can buy, are located in most towns and cities.*

Below: *A typical retail antique shop will usually display the furniture it has for sale in a sympathetic manner.*

ANTIQUE SHOPS

Most large towns will have at least one antique dealer, dealing in antique furniture of varying quality. Antique dealers generally fall into two categories – the trade dealer and the retailer – although some dealers may operate in both trade and retail areas.

The trade dealer, as the name suggests, deals mainly with other dealers. The stock will turn over fairly quickly and, as a result, will not be fully on display. The prices will often be a little lower than the retail dealer, but, should you decide to buy and seek "trade prices", then restoration, delivery costs and the facility to return goods are often excluded. While these can be arranged, you should expect to pay extra.

The other type of dealer is the retailer. Here the stock will be clearly labelled, suitably lit and well laid out. You will find that retailers are happy to spend as much time as you require answering all your questions and will often give you the option of trying the piece on approval. Delivery costs are normally included in the price, and the piece will already have been restored if necessary, with the dealer happy to explain what, if any, restoration work has been carried out. The retailer's goods may cost a little more than the trade dealer's, but it is worth remembering that in life one generally gets what one pays for.

Whoever you decide to deal with, it is best to find someone with whom you feel comfortable, who knows the field well and with whom you wish to do business. With regards to pricing, most dealers are open to negotiation within a limit, and you will soon learn what sort of price movement a dealer is happy to make. Good dealers often belong to a recognized trade association, which will have a strict code of practice and which can act as an arbiter in the case of any dispute.

ANTIQUE FAIRS

Antique fairs are becoming an increasingly popular way to purchase antiques, as they offer buyers the opportunity to view the stock belonging to many different dealers in just one day. They range from one-day fairs held in a local venue to large exhibitions held over several days in hotels or purpose-built exhibition centres, with the participating dealers building elaborate stands on which to display their pieces.

When visiting a fair, make sure you view everything before deciding upon your purchase, and take time to talk to the dealers, who will be happy to answer any questions you may have. If necessary, take details and measurements to check that a selected item is suitable. Some dealers may be happy for you to try the piece on approval. Often some of the best working relationships between a dealer and patron have begun at an antique fair.

Above: *Antique fairs are an ideal way to view a large selection of furniture in a single day.*

ON LINE

This is a comparatively new method of purchasing antiques, which has had varying degrees of success. Some major auction rooms have set up elaborate on-line auctions, but while such auctions seem to do well in some fields, with furniture it seems that people still like to see the piece "in the flesh", to try sitting in or at it and to examine it in all its aspects. The same is true of dealers' websites, which are proving to be more of a marketing tool than a retail point of sale.

Tools, equipment and materials

The right tools, equipment and materials are the lifeblood of

any restorer. Often passed from generation to generation,

they must be cared for and used with the skill they deserve,

for without them even the most gifted of restorers will be

unable to undertake the most basic of restoration jobs.

CREATING A WORKSPACE

More often than not, financial limitations and space will dictate the location of a workshop. The most important piece of equipment in the workshop will be the bench, so it is important that any area under consideration should, as a basic requirement, be able to house both you and the bench, as well as allowing space for the furniture being restored. You will also need to surround yourself with tools and machinery, so plan your work area carefully.

YOUR WORKBENCH

Once you have decided where to site your workbench, you will need to assess the various factors that are vital for good work.

The most important factor is the quality of light available. Natural light is ideal, so, if possible, position the bench directly under a window or skylight. Hang fluorescent strip lights above the workbench and, if you are intending to undertake any polishing work, make sure that normal lights are also available (fluorescent light gives a false colour). Also paint the walls white to reflect, and so maximize, whatever light there is.

Rack your tools in an organized manner so that they are readily available. Keep groups of tools, such as hammers, saws or chisels, together for easy access. Keep tools that are not used daily, such as carving tools, carefully wrapped to protect their sharp edges, and stored neatly ready for use. Above all, keep the work area and bench clean and tidy.

Remember that most of your time will be spent standing at the workbench, so put blocks under it, if necessary, to set it at a height that is comfortable for you to work at. Also, if possible, opt for a wooden rather than a concrete floor, as concrete is very tiring on the feet and legs.

If space and funds permit, have two separate areas within the workshop: one for cabinet making and the other, in a dust-free area, for polishing. This dual use maximizes the available space.

An ideal workbench

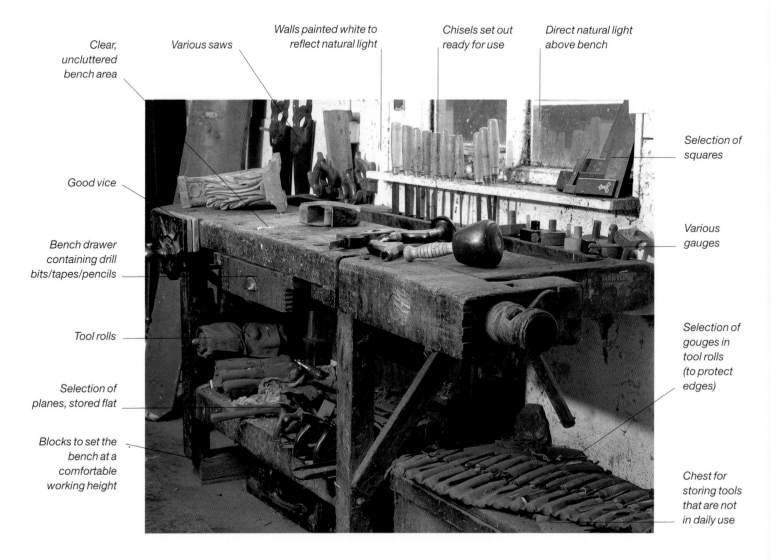

Clear, uncluttered bench area

Various saws

Walls painted white to reflect natural light

Chisels set out ready for use

Direct natural light above bench

Selection of squares

Good vice

Various gauges

Bench drawer containing drill bits/tapes/pencils

Tool rolls

Selection of gouges in tool rolls (to protect edges)

Selection of planes, stored flat

Blocks to set the bench at a comfortable working height

Chest for storing tools that are not in daily use

YOUR TOOLKIT

When restoring antique furniture, the best tools are, without doubt, those that were originally used in the 18th and 19th centuries. For a hobby restorer, modern tools are a suitable, and realistic, substitute, but anyone wishing to pursue a career in the field of furniture restoration should endeavour to build up as wide a collection of antique tools as possible. Such tools were made by craftsmen for craftsmen. The steel used then is still the best for holding a suitable cutting edge now, and the handles, made from box or rosewood, feel more comfortable to the hand than modern materials such as plastic. Often you will see numerous names stamped into the handle of an antique tool, indicating how it has passed through the hands of generations of craftsmen.

Old tools can be found in a number of places, ranging from specialized tool auctions or car boot sales, to local fêtes and classified advertisements in the local paper. If you are really lucky, you may have the opportunity to buy the tools and contents of the workshop of a retiring cabinet-maker. If this happens, beg or borrow the funds to buy the tools, since such events are rare indeed.

In the absence of antique tools, or while you are building up your collection, start your toolkit by buying modern equivalents, but be sure to buy the best quality that is available within your budget. Clamps are an exception to this rule, and modern sash, snap and G-clamps are fine. These are expensive pieces of equipment, so it is a good idea to buy a few whenever you can afford them.

Modern screwdrivers, saws and chisels can be purchased to begin with, and you can gradually replace them with older examples if you want. Some tools and equipment, such as spring clips, can be made in the workshop.

Most cabinet-makers take a lifetime to build up their collection of tools, and almost all craftsmen will prefer to work with only their own tools, which, once purchased, should last a lifetime.

If you become interested in restoring then you may become an avid collector of tools yourself. Certainly, if you decide to take up restoring as a job, then building up your stock of tools and materials can be seen as an investment in your own future. Remember always to respect your tools, keeping them clean and sharp, and wrapping them safely whenever they are not in use.

Safety

The safety rules of a workshop are esentially those of common sense. Always remember that the workshop is potentially a dangerous area, so make sure that children cannot get in. Always handle sharp tools with care and replace them in their rack after use. Keep a regularly tested fire extinguisher close to hand and lock any flammable materials away in a fireproof cabinet. Keep the work area clean and tidy and sweep up all shavings at the end of the day. Good ventilation is important, especially when using stripper or any other chemicals. Make sure any stains or other liquids are kept in jars and clearly labelled. Wear suitable safety clothing as the job dictates. Tie back long hair, remove any dangling jewellery and always wear a long apron to protect your clothes.

Above: *A fire extinguisher is essential. Install a powder-filled fire extinguisher at every exit door.*

Above: *When using power tools likely to create a lot of dust or sparks, it is a good idea to wear a protective helmet.*

Left: *Basic safety equipment should include a first-aid kit, goggles, ear defenders, a filter mask , gloves and a disposable mask.*

SAWS AND MEASURING DEVICES

It is important that saws are kept in good condition because a sharp edge is essential, particularly when doing detailed work. Although modern power saws can take much of the effort out of sawing, and certainly have their place in a workshop, hand-held saws, such as the tenon saw, are invaluable for small-scale work. Measuring devices, including dividers, callipers and gauges, are the key to successful cabinet work, so look after them carefully.

SAWS

The three most commonly used saws in day-to-day restoration are the full tenon saw, the half-tenon saw and the dovetail saw, all of which have varying numbers of teeth per centimetre (inch). The more teeth per centimetre (inch), the finer the cut will be. Some of the finest cutting teeth are those of the fret and coping saws, designed for detailed shape work.

The large panel saw, used for cutting larger boards, comes with two teeth settings: the cross cut, designed to cut across the grain, and the ripsaw, designed to cut along the length of the grain. With the introduction of modern band saws and circular saws, large panel saws are used less frequently, but all workshops should have at least one of each type.

Saws will almost certainly be used on a daily basis and should be used only for the specific task for which they were designed. Using a fine dovetail saw for general work, for example, will damage the teeth and make it unsuitable for the finer work of cutting dovetails.

The saw is a precision cutting tool and should always be kept sharp and in good condition. While it is possible to sharpen the saw yourself, it is far better to send it to a professional saw doctor to have the teeth set and sharpened.

Above: *An extensive range of reliable measuring tools is essential for the furniture restorer to carry out accurate work.*

When using a saw on a particularly difficult piece of wood, rub a little candle wax on the blade to help ease the cutting.

MEASURING DEVICES

"Measure twice, cut once" is an old cabinet-makers' saying, and it is as true today as it has always been. Accurate measuring is vital, since if the measuring is inaccurate then all the work that follows is wasted, at worst possibly leading to a ruined piece of valuable furniture, at best meaning you have to start all over again. Measuring tools include dividers, marking gauges, callipers, set (carpenter's) squares, sliding bevels and box rules, all of which are indispensable. Double-check every measurement and work from a face edge (the first edge cut and planed level, which is then used to take other measurements).

Left: *Three saws from a typical workshop, each with a different number of teeth per centimetre (inch). The more teeth a saw has, the finer the cut will be.*

Hammers and Screwdrivers

Hammers, ranging from pin hammers for light work to heavier hammers for knocking apart furniture, are an essential part of any restoration work, as are the various types of mallet, particularly the carver's dummy, which is a very useful tool. A wide range of screwdrivers should also be kept to hand. Look out for examples with long and short shanks, which are useful in different situations. Be sure to keep the leading edge of a screwdriver sharp.

HAMMERS

The restorer will have two or three different types in the workshop, including the light pin hammer, the general cabinet hammer, which will be used on a daily basis, and a heavier hammer used to knock apart carcasses and drive in large nails. Hammers should never be used to hit another tool, such as a chisel – that is exclusively the role of the mallet.

When the face of a hammer becomes dirty and worn, file it flat then rub it lightly with fine-grade sandpaper to remove the dirt and score the surface. This enables the hammer to grip the head of the nail. This process, which is known as "dressing", will probably need to be done at least two or three times a month.

MALLETS

These were designed to be used against the handle of a tool such as a chisel or gouge. They come in different weights and shapes, and the greater the weight of the head, the more force it will exert. A good example of this is the carver's dummy, whose heavy lignum vitae head

Above: *Two traditional mallets – it is useful to have a selection in your workshop.*

ensures that a simple wrist action gives a very strong blow. It also means that the carver need not look at the mallet as it swings down, since its rounded head will always strike the tool being used, thus allowing the carver to concentrate fully on the work in hand.

Larger mallets are for roughing off, while lighter ones are for delicate work. The square-headed mallet is for general cabinet work and knocking apart, where a large hammer might bruise the wood.

SCREWDRIVERS

It is best to equip yourself with as wide a range of screwdrivers as possible. It is well worth spending a little time at car boot sales or trawling through second-hand shops in order to build a collection of traditional tools at a lower price than new ones. Old screwdrivers tend to have a longer shank, which gives better leverage. They also have handles made from box-wood or beech, which are kinder to the hand than plastic. Small screwdrivers with short shanks can be very useful for removing screws in awkward locations.

When buying an old screwdriver, check that the leading edge is straight and even. If it is worn or uneven, you will have to grind it flush, because a screwdriver that does not fit snugly into a screw-head slot can break the screw. Remember that a screwdriver is designed for removing and putting in screws and should never be used as a lever, which could damage the edge and bend the shank.

Below: *A selection of old screwdrivers with shanks of varying lengths.*

Holding a hammer

1 *When using a hammer, the most common mistake is to hold it half way down the handle in the belief that this allows more control and accuracy. In fact, it has the opposite effect.*

2 *The correct way to hold the hammer is at the end of its handle, which gives much better balance and control. When using a hammer, make several medium blows rather than trying to drive the nail home first time.*

SMOOTHING TOOLS AND CLAMPS

There are many different types of planes and clamps used in restoration work, and modern tools are very similar to their traditional counterparts. Some planes are fitted with their own guide fences and others with changeable blades, while moulding planes have specially shaped bases and blades for detailed shaping work. Different clamps, like planes, are designed for particular tasks and it is advisable to build up as wide a selection as possible.

PLANES

The earliest planes were made with wood bodies, but during the 18th and 19th centuries the metal-bodied plane took over, although the moulding planes remained wooden.

There are various examples of planes, each suited to a particular role, including the utilitarian jack plane, the smoothing plane, and the smaller block-and-shoulder plane for more intricate work. There are also specialized planes, such as moulding planes, with their specially shaped bases and blades, which are designed to cut the waist, base and other mouldings found on carcass furniture. However, the modern router, with its wide range of shaped cutters, has largely taken over this role. Although the spokeshave does not look like a plane, it is classed as one because it works along the same principle.

The blade of any plane is designed to cut the wood cleanly without tearing the grain, and so it is important that it is always kept sharp. When the blade is sharp and the plane is used correctly, it should made a wonderful slicing sound as it cuts through the wood.

SCRAPERS

The cabinet scraper, which is basically a piece of metal with a burred edge, is designed to clean up surfaces and remove any plane marks prior to sanding.

The most frequently used scraper will be a rectangular one for shaped mouldings, but tailor-made scrapers are also useful. The most common example is the French curve, which is shaped like a kidney and should be able to scrape any concave area.

Scrapers should always be used sharp and should produce shavings, not dust. To sharpen a scraper, you should draw a hard piece of rounded metal, such as the shank of a screwdriver, across the edge. This produces a burr, which is needed to cut the wood.

SANDING EQUIPMENT

The earliest types of sandpaper were, in fact, made from sharkskin, known as shagreen. It was dried and used very much in the same way as sandpaper is today. This was followed by the use of ground glass or sand, which was stuck to paper, and it is from this that the terms "glasspaper" and "sandpaper" are derived.

Nowadays there are many abrasive papers available, including silicon carbide, aluminium oxide and garnet paper, but the term "sandpaper" is still commonly used to describe them all. These papers are available in a number of different grits, or grades, with the most commonly used grits in the workshop ranging from 80 (the coarsest) to 320 (the finest).

Sandpaper is rarely used on its own but is wrapped around sanding blocks of cork or wood. If a specific moulding has to be sanded, you will need to make a shaped piece of wood (overloe) that matches the profile of the moulding, so that it can be sanded without having its shape altered. Over the years, the restorer will build up a wide selection of tailor-made overloes.

When you start sandpapering a piece of work, begin with the coarsest grade and work up through the grades to the finest. Wetting the wood between each grade, and allowing it to dry before you start with the next grade, will give a smoother finish. Also, if you intend to apply a water stain, this inter-grade wetting process will make sure that the grain does not rise at the staining stage.

Above: *A selection of planes showing some of the variety of shapes and materials used in their construction.*

Above: *The spokeshave is a cross between a plane and a scraper, and is a very versatile tool for shaping wood.*

Above: *Overloes are specially shaped wooden blocks that are used with sandpaper to smooth the profile of a moulding.*

CLAMPS

These tools come in a wide variety of styles, each suited to a particular role. The most common types are the long sash clamp, the G-clamp, which comes in different sizes, the band clamp, the snap clamp and the spring clip. Modern clamps are similar to traditional ones, and although they are fairly expensive to buy, it is best to build up as wide a range as possible.

When working with clamps, always use clamping blocks to prevent bruising and the appearance of "hoof" marks on the wood. Also, never over-tighten a clamp: the pressure it exerts can cause structural damage to delicate pieces.

When gluing up a complex job, it is a good idea to have a "dry" run beforehand, working out which clamps will be used and in which order. Spending a little time doing this may prevent problems later on

when the glue has been applied and is setting. It also means that you will have everything you need to hand and will feel confident about starting the work.

Above: *A wide selection of modern and traditional clamps, including G-clamps and sash clamps, are essential for many types of restoration work.*

Making a band clamp

While most clamps can be bought, the steel band clamp is unique in that it is workshop made and tailored to a particular job in hand. Its role is to clamp an oval or round, creating an equal pressure around the circumference.

You will need a small block of hardwood, a steel band (as used for binding building materials), small screws and a clamp.

1 *Cut two lengths of the steel band to a length slightly shorter than the frame's circumference and punch two pilot holes into each end of them.*

2 *Using a metal bit, drill two small holes through the pilot holes. Be sure to place a scrap block of wood on the bench or worktop to protect it.*

3 *Use a countersink drill bit to countersink the two holes previously drilled. This will make sure that the screw heads are level with the band.*

4 *After marking the shape of the frame on the hardwood, use a band saw to cut the concave profile. Cut the block in half.*

5 *Screw the two lengths of steel band to the shaped side of the hardwood, making sure that the countersunk hole side of the band is used.*

6 *Finish by filing the screw heads flush with the metal band, this will make sure that no unnecessary scratching or marking occurs.*

7 *The band clamp in use. The hardwood blocks are clamped together to create the tension.*

CHISELS AND CARVING TOOLS

All these implements have their own jobs, which involve paring away wood in one form or another, but one rule applicable to all is to keep their edges sharp so that they can cut through wood and not tear the grain. If you are interested in carving, you will start to amass a large collection of tools, since each has its own specific function. In general, old examples tend to keep their edge longer than modern versions, due to the better-quality steel.

CHISELS

The cabinet-maker or restorer will have three main types of chisel to hand on the workbench. These are the paring chisel, the mortise chisel and the firmer chisel. Within these groupings there should be a range of widths suitable for any task.

The paring chisel, with its bevelled edges and long blade, is primarily used for paring, levelling and chamfering. It is designed for hand-use only and should never be struck with a mallet.

The mortise chisel, as its name suggests, is used to cut out mortises, and for this reason its blade is noticeably thicker than that of both the paring and firmer chisels. The thickness of the blade means that it can withstand a heavy blow from a mallet and a certain amount of leverage when removing the waste wood from a mortise.

The firmer chisel, with its shorter, thicker blade without a bevelled side, is designed for heavier work and can be used in conjunction with a suitable mallet.

CARVING TOOLS

The carver is one of the most skilled craftspeople in the field of antique restoration. The skill of carving is similar to that of a painter, except that the carver's medium is wood and the end results are three-dimensional.

The required tools, which can number into the thousands, are known individually for their suitabilities and strengths, and before undertaking a carving project the carver will select the required implements and sharpen them. Indeed, depending on the hardness of the wood, it is not unknown for a carver to resharpen a blade every few minutes during carving work.

Small carving tools are essential for detailed and intricate work. They provide much greater control of the task in hand, allowing the carver to remove small slivers of wood with the minimum of effort.

There are numerous types of carving tools, including scrolls, which set out the shape of the carving; V- or parting tools, which produce long sweeps; grounders,

Above: *While gradually building up a collection of antique tools, which you can find in second-hand shops, it is a good idea to purchase modern equivalents too.*

which remove the background waste; veiners, which carve the fine details, such as flowers, leaves, etc; and fish tails, which, like the grounders, help to remove unwanted wood.

While this procedure may seem very complicated, it is worth noting that the complexity and intricacy of much of the work means that it takes several years for a carver to reach full potential.

Each carving project can often take hundreds of hours of painstaking work, and, aside from patience, the main skill a potential carver needs to learn is the ability to be able to study an existing carving closely and to mimic exactly the hand in which it was originally carved. The real test of the master carver is to restore carving to the extent that the new work blends in seamlessly with the original detail.

Left: *A selection of chisels, gouges and bradawls (for making fine pilot holes) will be used on a daily basis.*

Left: *A small selection of the many hundreds of carving tools required by the master carver.*

Above: *A carver's vice allows free and easy access to any carved piece held in it.*

Sharpening a chisel

Some of the tools most used by the cabinet-maker or furniture restorer are the various chisels. These are used to pare, level and shape the wood. It is vital that the chisels are kept sharp at all times, as failure to do so will result in them tearing the grain rather than slicing through the wood. When a chisel loses its edge, the process of re-honing takes only a few minutes, and the procedure is very simple.

1 *Using a grinding wheel and selecting the finest grade of the two stones, offer the chisel at an angle of approximately 25–30 degrees. Remove the bevel as soon as it is flat, otherwise the chisel's length will be shortened too much and its working life substantially reduced.*

2 *Lightly lubricate an oil stone with a fine oil, then draw the chisel repeatedly along the stone at an angle of 30–35 degrees. This will produce the cutting edge.*

3 *Turn the chisel over and lay it flat down on the stone. Rub it back and forth two or three times. This process, known as "backing off", will weaken the burr that has built up. Strop the chisel on a piece of leather, which should remove the burr.*

4 *Finally, use your newly sharpened chisel to cut a slither off a piece of wood. This will check for sharpness as well as removing the burr, should it not have come off on the leather strop.*

5 *The illustration shows how the finished edge should look if the chisel has been sharpened correctly.*

MACHINERY

While antique restoration is traditionally a craft that relies on hand-held tools, the use of machinery can, in certain cases, make life much easier. It was the mass introduction of mechanized tools during the 19th century that radically altered furniture production. Although they can never replace the trained craftsman, the new generation of hand-held power tools available today will certainly save you many valuable hours in the workshop.

The use of heavy machinery in the restoration workshop is fairly limited. In fact, not many restoration workshops will have the space for a fully fitted machine shop, especially as the heavier types often require three-phase electricity supplies. (This involves installing a unit to boost the power from single to three phase, and is usually needed only in commercial workshops.) However, the inclusion of certain heavy machines can make life much easier, and two invaluable machines are the band saw and the lathe.

Hand-held machine tools, such as an electric or cordless drill, jigsaw and router, are a great help, and you should stock as wide a range of router cutters as possible. You could also buy a router bench, which extends the possibilities of the router. As finances and space allow, you can buy extra machinery, such as circular saws, thickness planers and pillar drills. While these will not be used on a daily basis, they can save hours of effort when they are required. As with all machinery, it is vital that you obtain the correct training before using it (see Further Information, p.93) and that you always carefully follow the safety instructions.

BAND SAW

The band saw's blade is a flexible length of steel that runs in a continuous loop. It is ideal for cutting curves and angles or for trimming strips from wider pieces. Its limitations are governed by the depth of the sawbed and the thickness of the blade. Never apply undue pressure to the blade, as this will damage it or the guiding rollers and cause it to snap.

As a general rule, allow the saw to cut at its own speed. Any excessive force will be indicated by the driving motors straining and starting to slow down.

band saw

lathe

LATHE

The lathe allows you to accomplish a wide variety of tasks, ranging from the turning of legs, bobbins, bead mouldings and spindles to the copying of handles and decorative roundels or paterae.

Due to the speed and torque at which lathes operate, a lathe with a heavy cast body is ideal for restoration work, as this will counter any vibration. It is essential to take an approved instructional course in lathe work before you start using one as misuse can result in serious injury.

router

router bench

jigsaw

electric drill

ROUTER

The router is an extremely versatile hand tool. Its shaped cutter rotates at high speeds and will, if used correctly, give a clean, even cut. It can also be used with a guide fence or depth stop, and the range of cutters available is immense. Care should be taken in its use: no loose clothing should be worn, hair should be tied back and eye protection should be worn.

ROUTER BENCH

The router bench allows the router to be mounted upside down and so converted into a spindle moulder. The bench should always be used with guide fences and safety guards. The bench can often be dismantled, allowing for convenient storage when not in use.

POWER DRILLS

Cordless and electric drills are both ideal machines for workshop use. While you may sometimes require the use of a more traditional hand drill, such as when undertaking delicate work that may need to be executed one turn of the drill bit at a time, a power drill is one of the few modern tools that is preferred over the old version. Always buy the best model possible and, in the case of a cordless drill, always have the spare battery on charge ready to be changed over. These drills can also be used with screwdriver heads, although this would, of course, be for more general use and not for fine antique work, since the brass and steel antique screw heads would break if a power drill were used on them. Both types of drill can be used with a variety of bits and will accomplish a multitude of tasks. A drill stand can also be purchased to allow the drill to be used as a pillar drill.

cordless drill

JIGSAW

The jigsaw has a blade with a rise and fall action that cuts through sheet wood with ease. While it is not suitable for fine work, it is ideal for roughing out or cutting shaped templates (patterns) when the pieces are too large to fit into a band saw. Remember that the blade passes through the wood and continues to cut below, so care should be taken when using this tool.

COLLECTING AND STORING WOOD

A supply of suitable wood is an essential aspect of a restorer's workshop, and different kinds must be sourced, collected and properly stored. To the casual observer, such a collection of pieces of wood, salvaged from previous centuries of furniture making, may seem little more than firewood, but to the antique furniture restorer they are a priceless commodity, as without them his or her task would be impossible to undertake.

The aim of every restorer is, wherever possible, to restore a piece of furniture without trace. To do this requires the use of old surface woods and veneers that match the original as closely as possible in colour and grain. Also, when missing mouldings have to be remade, the material used must be of the same type as the original in order to make a good repair.

Two woods in constant demand by restorers are Cuban and Honduras mahogany, which, during the 18th century, were the woods of choice for furniture making. Both are now nearly impossible to buy from any wood merchant, and so any old examples found must be bought and put away until needed. This shows the vital importance of the restorer's "breaker store".

The breaker store, as the name so graphically describes, is a collection of pieces of antique furniture that have been bought not to be restored but to be carefully knocked apart, sorted into the various woods and stacked away for future reuse in the restoration of better pieces. Such an example might be a collection of quarter-sawn oak drawer sides, waiting to be used in the repair or replacement of a missing drawer, or perhaps an old Cuban mahogany table leaf, long ago separated from its table, waiting to be used in the making of a missing bracket foot or to be reshaped with a moulding plane to replace a missing section of top moulding.

The source of breakers is endless, and no opportunity should be missed to scour junk shops, local auctions or even skips. An old Victorian chest bought for very little indeed could provide enough oak

linings, Cuban mahogany and even old locks to pay for itself many times over. Building a comprehensive breaker store can be a lifetime's work, and a useful tip to keep a store expanding is that every time some wood is used from the store, it should be replaced with more wood than was taken out. Indeed, it is a prerequisite for application to the antique restorers' most senior trade organization, The British Antique Furniture Restorers' Association (BAFRA), that the applicant is able to demonstrate the active building-up of a collection of breakers.

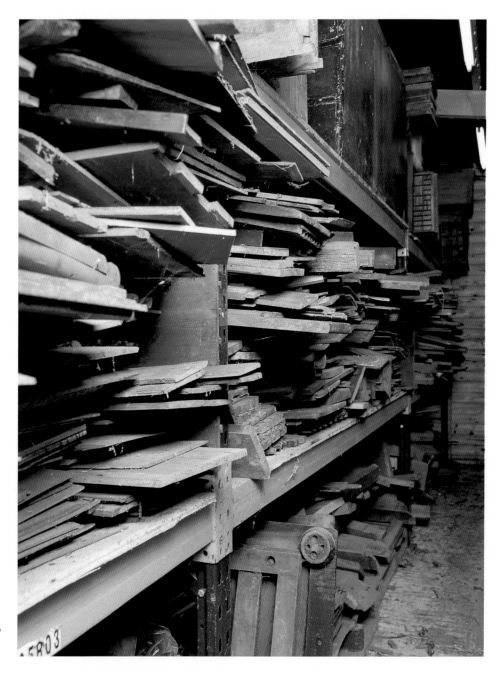

Right: *A well-stocked and logically arranged breaker store will supply a restorer with wood to match virtually any restoration project.*

The breaker store should be racked and labelled and the woods stored in the various marked sections. This saves both time and effort when searching for a particular piece and enables the restorer to see which, if any, types of veneer are running low or are not represented at all.

Any veneers should be removed from their wood core (see p.24) and stored separately in a veneer store. Any nails and screws should also be removed, partly for potential reuse if they are in good condition and partly as a method of preventing any unnecessary scratching from occurring. The store should be kept dry but not overly so, as excessive heat will cause the woods to warp and split, creating as much damage as dampness.

While the majority of woods will be old, if an opportunity arises it is a good idea to buy some modern woods, such as walnut, yew or oak for renovating country-made pieces. These should then be professionally cut into boards, stacked so that air can circulate freely between them and allowed to dry and season naturally under cover.

If, however, space will not allow this storage, and modern wood has to be purchased when needed, remember that it is always better to buy air-dried rather than kiln-dried wood, as the former will be more stable in the long term.

To the untrained eye, a restorer's breaker store may look like a confused jumble of wood. The owner, however, will know all the stock that is there, even wood that was acquired years ago. When a particular grain or surface is needed, the restorer should be able to locate it almost immediately, recalling it from the day it was placed there. Next to tools, an extensive and expanding supply of breakers is one of the most important considerations for a furniture restorer.

Below: *An example of the numerous repairs for which the components of a breaker chest can be used.*

Veneer used for patching small areas of damaged or missing veneer

Solid mahogany sides used for making bracket feet, mouldings, etc

Handles and locks used as replacements for missing ones

Oak drawer sides used for replacement sides or damaged drawers

Old surface pine from carcass used for patching old surfaces, etc

COLLECTING AND STORING VENEERS

While early furniture was made using solid wood, by the late 17th century the use of veneer was becoming more widespread. Originally cut by saw, by the latter part of the 19th century thinner (and therefore cheaper) veneers were cut by peeling the log, a technique known as "knife cut", which increased their use still further. Whenever possible, a comprehensive store of used and new veneer should be stocked.

Veneers, like breakers (see p.22), are an important commodity for any serious-minded restorer. While good veneer merchants will hold a comprehensive stock of various cuts of veneer, it is still a good idea for the restorer, wherever possible, to compile a separate store in a shed or unused room. This veneer store should include not only new veneers, which may be bought in bundles, often held together with string, but also old surface veneers, which may have been removed from breakers.

With time, the colour of certain woods can alter greatly from their original colour, and for this reason the furniture restorer should aim to collect as wide a range of old surface veneers as possible.

Left: *A selection of bandings and stringings, which are often used in veneer work, are useful. They can be purchased from good veneer merchants.*

Before being stored, old surface veneers will need to be removed from their core. A damp cloth is placed on top of the veneer and is then heated with an iron. The resulting steam softens the original animal glue, allowing the veneer to be gently eased off. This is done by sliding a flat-bladed knife between the veneer and the core. The old glue should be washed from the back of the veneer with hot water while it is still sticky.

The veneer should then be placed between two sheets of paper and have pressure applied to it. A hand veneer press is ideal for this, but alternatively the veneer can be placed between two flat pieces of wood with weights placed on top. This will allow the veneer to dry flat.

When the veneer is dry, it can be sorted with any other new pieces and then placed in the veneer store. Long lengths should be stored flat on slatted wood shelving, which allows the air to circulate freely. Smaller pieces, which can be used to repair

cross bandings or inlays, can be placed in shoe boxes. The storage shed or room should not be allowed to become too dry, because this will cause the veneers to shrink and split. If possible, a slightly damp and cool atmosphere is best, because this allows the veneers to remain malleable. Laying cardboard on top of the veneer will also stop it becoming too dry and brittle.

Selecting a particular veneer from the store is a task best carried out by two people, one at each end of the veneer bundles, so that they can turn the bundles evenly as they search for the exact match. This method should prevent any unnecessary damage to the bundles. If, however, a veneer develops a split that starts to travel up its length, secure this with a piece of brown parcel tape.

When a piece of veneer has been removed from a shelf, the remaining pieces should be replaced in the same order as they were originally stacked. Failure to do so could result in different veneers being stacked together, which would then make selecting a particular veneer much harder in the future.

Left: *Any veneer store should be racked to allow the veneers to lie flat and be easily and quickly identified.*

COLOUR AND PATINATION

Without doubt, the two most important aspects to any antique furniture are those of colour and patination. People often think that the two are the same, but in fact both are different, as each term refers to a different aspect of the finish found in antique furniture. It is the glorious colour and surface patination that furniture develops that the buyer and collector both seek. And their presence, or at times their absence, can radically alter the value of a particular piece.

Colour

The colour of a piece is found in the actual surface of the wood. This surface area illustrates how the wood has reacted over the years as many generations of natural light have affected its surface. It is interesting that for numerous reasons two pieces of the same wood, such as Cuban mahogany, can react in different ways. This can depend on the amount of light a piece has been exposed to or how dense a particular grain is. Also, a solid rounded piece, such as a chair upright, will react differently to a flat area, such as a chest top. Veneer will also change its appearance in a different way to a piece of solid wood.

Different woods can also be changed quite markedly over time, for instance kingwood and rosewood are both very purple when first cut and polished, but become a golden colour after many years of exposure. The change in mahogany, which when first polished has a very red tone, ranges from dark nutty brown to light honey colour. It is this variation that makes each piece of antique furniture unique. Unfortunately, this colour can easily be ruined by over-zealous cleaning, which allows chemicals to alter the tones, colours and hues of the wood. It is worth remembering that once altered, the original colour cannot be returned.

Patination

The term patination can best be described as the history of a piece mirrored in its surface colour and shine. Technically, it is caused by generations of oxidation of the polished surface, combined with a build-

Above and below: These photographs illustrate the inner and outer surface of an 18th-century tea table. The inner surface, which has spent its lifetime closed and protected from the effects of light, has kept the original red colour (top). In contrast, the top of the table has mellowed and, after generations of waxing, has developed a magnificent patinated surface (below). This is an example of mahogany colour and patination at its best.

up of furniture waxes, natural grease and dust. Its appearance can be altered by many factors, including sunlight, the amount of waxing a piece has received in its lifetime, whether any solvents have been applied and the type of finish originally used when the piece was made. For example, the patination found on a piece of mid-18th-century mahogany, which would have been polished with oil, varies greatly from that found on an early 18th-century piece of walnut, which would have been finished with varnish and wax. While good patination is often present on good pieces of furniture, truly great patination is rare. When it is present, therefore, every effort should be made to maintain it.

VENEERS AND WOOD

It is the sheer variety of the woods and veneers used in their construction that makes furniture, both antique and modern, so pleasing. During previous centuries, as new woods were discovered and imported, it allowed cabinet-makers and designers to explore new techniques and designs utilizing the qualities unique to these woods. The opening up of the world in terms of trade can be directly linked to changes in furniture design over the centuries.

Left: *The tools used for cutting and laying veneer are fairly basic and have remained unaltered throughout the centuries.*

During the 16th century, almost all furniture was still made from solid wood. By the latter part of the 17th century, however, veneer began to play an increasingly important role in furniture making. Some changes in construction techniques followed, and in certain pieces the carcass was now little more than a framework on which to apply the veneer. Dutch, French and Italian furniture-makers experimented with marquetry and parquetry designs, while others began to use native woods such as walnut and elm – all which had formerly been used in the solid – in veneer form to gain the maximum benefit from the beauty of the grain and natural burr patterns. These same burrs, which would have been far too unstable to appear in solid wood furniture (they have a natural tendency to split and twist during seasoning after construction), could now be cut into thinner veneers and applied on to a stable core carcass of oak.

The first veneers were cut by hand. This was laborious and meant that the veneers were thick and fairy expensive to produce, but as quality furniture was still a luxury commodity, it mattered little. With the use of industrial machinery during the 19th century came thinner and cheaper veneers. These veneers allowed previously expensive woods such as mahogany and satinwood to be incorporated into a wider range of furniture.

How veneers are cut

To slice veneers from a log, the log is mounted in a frame that rotates or slides up and down against a sharp blade. Depending on the way the log is mounted, different sections of the figure in the grain can be displayed to their best effect.

Rotary-cut veneers follow the growth rings in the log as it is unpeeled like a giant roll of paper. They are produced in large sizes.

Flat-cut, or crown cut, veneers are cut parallel to the centre line of the log. Woods with distinct growth lines are best sliced in this way.

Quarter-cut veneers are cut at right angles through the rings. This displays the rays in wide bands, as in quartered oak, with its distinctive silvery "flash" rays.

Rift cut, or comb cut, veneers are cut with the blade offset at a slight angle from the quarter position. This produces a fine parallel grain figure.

Types of veneer cuts

One advantage of using veneers over solid wood, which was quickly appreciated by the cabinet-maker, was that each individual tree as well as each species of tree could produce examples of many different types of patterns. This allowed the cabinet-maker and furniture designer to break up an expanse of wood with patterns and designs that are both unique and highly decorative.

However, although no two pieces of veneer are exactly alike, they can be categorized into broad types, depending on from which part of the tree they come from and their general pattern and form.

CURL VENEER

A curl veneer is obtained by cutting from the fork of the tree where the trunk divides. It gives a feathering effect, and in woods such as mahogany was highly sought after for drawer fronts and tops. Mahogany curl veneer was particularly popular during the 18th and 19th centuries.

BURR VENEER

The burr is found on the side of the trunk where numerous growths have occurred. Often found near the bottom of the tree, they are sometimes known as burr clusters. Usually only available in small sections, they are unstable until glued to a stable core.

BUTT VENEER

This veneer, as the name suggests, is taken from the root, or butt, of the tree. Dense in grain, it is often wild in figure with much swirling movement.

FIDDLE VENEER

This prized veneer was used in the manufacture of violins, hence its name. It has a distinctive stripe, which usually runs at right angles to the grain, and was favoured during the 18th century with mahogany and stained sycamore, known as harewood.

FIGURED VENEER

Not as wild as burr but still with movement, this type of veneer was popular in the making of quarter-veneered tops and bookmatched ends. Various theories abound as to why some veneers are more figured than others, but it is this variety that creates uniqueness.

OYSTER VENEER

The oyster veneer, which is obtained by slicing through the branch to give distinctive rings, was popular during the 17th and early 18th centuries from woods such as olive, walnut and laburnum. It was usually then enhanced with geometric line inlays of box or holly.

Veneer treatments

Although it is possible for veneers to be simply applied in sheet form, it is far more usual for them to be laid in decorative patterns. The range of patterns is fairly small and will often be dictated by the type of cut of veneer and the origin or date of the piece. When these veneer patterns are laid, it is important that the sheets of veneer are selected from the same bundle, and indeed in the same order in which they were cut, otherwise the pattern can seem disjointed.

QUARTER-VENEERED

As the name suggests, this is the design where the top is veneered in a quarter pattern radiating out from the centre. The most popular cut used is the figured veneer, although the use of burr is also known. Quarter-veneers were often bordered with further crossbanding to form a frame. During the 19th century, round tops were veneered in numerous curls that radiated toward the centre, but this was known as segmented veneering.

BOOKMATCHED

The bookmatched veneer surface is obtained by taking two subsequent veneer sheets from a bundle, opening them out and laying them next to each other so that they form a counter pattern, rather like the wings of a butterfly. This is done with figured veneer and can be found on the sides or fronts of chests or bureaux, or perhaps on the top of a centre table.

BLOCKED

This technique was used during the 17th century, especially on the ends of marquetry chests. It allowed a patterned centre to be veneered around quickly and meant that odd cuts of a veneer could be used when a pattern would make it difficult to cut around. (Marquetry panels were laid prior to the surrounding veneer being applied.)

FEATHERED

In this method the veneer is cut and laid at an angle. Although quite rare, it is found on certain 18th- and 19th-century pieces of quality to give a decorative treatment to a door.

SCARF-JOINTED

This technique is used when a straight edge is not possible or desirable, for example when using burr veneers that come in small pieces. While they may be cut straight along the quartered line, the joints connecting the various pieces should remain hidden to give the illusion that each quarter is in fact one piece rather than a number of pieces joined together. A wavy cut is made that should be lost in the swirl of the grain. Over time, the veneer may shrink a little due to seasoning and the joints may become visible again.

Types of veneer

Like solid wood, veneers are affected by the action of light, polish and wax. Indeed, the range of colours found in veneer can be quite marked, and it is these colours, tones and hues that are so readily sought after today by the collector.

Although the types of woods used are numerous, and choice very much depends on the origin and date of the piece, the majority of popular antiques today use the woods illustrated in the following sections.

MAHOGANY

Numerous types of mahogany are available, but the two most commonly used for furniture manufacture during the 18th and 19th centuries were Cuban (*Swietenia mahogoni*) and Honduras mahogany (*Swietenia macrophylla*). With its rich red colour and dense hard grain, this solid wood was ideal for furniture manufacture. When cut into veneer form, the mahogany was highly decorative, especially when the sought-after curls were used in the door panels of bookcases or linen presses.

Above: *Cuban mahogany veneer prior to use and polishing.*

Above: *A Cuban mahogany curl veneer panel having mellowed and patinated to a wonderful surface.*

Above: *A George III linen press, c.1790, veneered in well-figured Cuban mahogany throughout and with curl veneer panels.*

WALNUT

European walnut (*Juglans regia*) was widely used for furniture manufacture from the 17th century onward, and by the end of that century its use in veneer form was increasingly fashionable for finer pieces.

Although indigenous to warmer European climates, such as France, Italy and Turkey, it was also produced in England. The Great Frost of 1709 destroyed most of the European trees, and so its export from France was banned after 1720.

Its use in furniture in veneer form declined during the 18th century, but it become popular again during the mid-19th century. When first polished, it is almost orange, but it will mellow to either a honey colour or a rich nutty one.

Right: *A walnut veneer.*

Right: *A walnut veneer after 300 years of waxing.*

Above: *An 18th-century walnut-veneered bureau of excellent colour and patination.*

ROSEWOOD

This wood comes in two forms: Indian rosewood (*Dalbergia latifolia*) and Brazilian rosewood (*Dalbergia nigra*). During the 18th century, Indian rosewood was more commonly used in the solid in Indian and Anglo-Indian furniture, while Brazilian rosewood was more favoured in veneer form during the 19th century. It is often seen on table tops laid on to a mahogany core. While deep purple when first polished, rosewood mellows to a rich warm tone and on occasion can even become golden brown in colour.

Right: *A Brazilian rosewood veneer.*

Right: *A Brazilian rosewood veneer that has developed a rich colour.*

Above: *A Regency centre table, c.1815, veneered in well-figured Brazilian rosewood and inlaid with brass.*

SATINWOOD

West Indian satinwood (*Zanthoxylum flavum*) originates from the Caribbean islands, while East Indian satinwood (*Chloroxylon swietenia*) comes from southern India and Sri Lanka. The wood was not in demand for furniture making until the mid-18th century. Although it was sometimes used in solid form during the latter part of the 19th century, it was mainly used in decorative veneer form. East Indian satinwood, which can be seen on later 19th-century pieces, is richer in colour than the West Indian variety and often has a characteristic ribbon stripe when the veneer is quarter cut. It is yellow when first polished, but develops a golden rich colour over time.

Right: *A piece of West Indian veneer when first cut.*

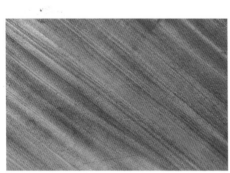

Right: *A West Indian veneer that has mellowed and patinated to a golden yellow/orange colour.*

Right: *A George III game and work table, c.1785, veneered in West Indian satinwood.*

OAK

There are more than 300 varieties of oak, but European and English oak are the same species – *Quercus robur*. Until the 17th century, most furniture was made from oak. However, as the century progressed, newly imported woods became fashionable and oak was largely downgraded to either internal carcass work or country-made pieces. When first cut it is a light honey colour, and if quarter sawn it will show its distinctive, silvery, medullary ray figure, but after initial waxing it can become much darker and will continue to darken over time.

Right: *Oak when first cut, with its light golden colour.*

Right: *With time and generations of waxing, a rich warm tone will develop.*

Above: *An early 19th-century sarcophagus wine cooler veneered in burr oak.*

POLISHES AND GLUES

One of the most attractive features of antique furniture is its distinctive grain patterns. It is the application of polish and waxes that, while helping to protect, feed and nourish the wood, also enhances its appearance.

The polishes and techniques used today are nearly identical to those used for generations before, although the restorers of old would have had to make their own polish recipes as well as making all their own glues.

POLISHES

Ever since wooden furniture was first made, its grain has been sealed in one way or another. Waxes were used to burnish the surface, and, during the 17th century, varnishes were applied that helped to protect and enhance the wood. During the 19th century, a new technique was adopted that resulted in a shellac polish, made from the shells of lac beetles, being applied with a cotton and linen pad known as a rubber (see pp.60–61). This sealed the grain, protected the wood and brought out the pattern and figure of popular imported woods such as mahogany, satinwood and rosewood.

The polisher's basic requirements are few. The equipment involves wadding (batting) and linen or other lint-free cloth for making rubbers, a selection of various grades of wire (steel) wool, as well as a wide selection of various brushes and some mutton cloth for buffing surfaces.

The polisher's materials include shellac polish, which can be bought in either liquid form or as shellac flakes to be

mixed with spirit (alcohol), and is kept in a glass or plastic bottle. Various coloured pigments to be mixed with water or spirit are needed for tinting or colouring repairs, and stopping waxes, again in various shades, are also needed. The final material is methylated spirits (methyl alcohol), which should be stored in a fire-proof cabinet. All the above equipment and materials can be obtained from a good trade supplier.

One of the main attractions of an antique piece of furniture is its colour and, hopefully, its patinated surface, so great care should be taken whenever polish is applied. The skill of the polisher is to revive a surface by gently removing the perished layers and then rebuilding the surface layer by layer. Work on small areas should be kept as localized as possible so as not to affect the surrounding areas.

Above: *Brushes, polishes and stains are needed for nearly every restoration job. Keep a good selection to hand.*

Patience and practice are therefore the watchwords. A good eye for colour is also needed to ensure that patches and repairs blend in with the surroundings areas. They should be practically invisible. It is also essential to have an understanding of traditional techniques and materials and to know when to clean a piece and when it is better to leave it alone. Over-zealous cleaning will not only spoil the aesthetic appearance but will almost certainly devalue the piece considerably.

Professionally, a polisher may take many years to learn the craft, and, without doubt, the polisher's role in a workshop is every bit as important as that of the cabinet-maker or restorer.

Above: *Rubbers should be kept in an air-tight jar or tin to stop them drying out.*

GLUES

Until the 15th and early 16th centuries, very little glue was used in the manufacture of furniture. Instead, the joints were held together with pegs or crude, hand-made clout nails. By the 17th century, however, as furniture construction became more complex and designs and styles more adventurous, animal glues were being employed in furniture making.

While new adhesives have been developed over the years, animal glues are still the most frequently used glues in furniture restoration. The sight and smell of the glue pot in any workshop is the same today as it was in the 17th, 18th and 19th centuries, and putting it on the fire or hot plate is still the apprentice's first task every morning.

Three main types of glue are used in the modern workshop: animal glue, PVA (white) glue and cascamite. Each has its own role and will be selected according to the nature of the required join.

Animal glue

This glue is made today as it has been for the last 300 years: animal feet and skin are boiled and the resulting liquid is poured into cold water, causing it to crystallize into small pearls. These pearls can then be mixed with water and allowed to soak overnight, before being heated in a special glue pot to melt them.

Above: *Animal glue is applied hot, using a bristle brush.*

Above: *The three most commonly used glues today (clockwise from top): animal glue, PVA (white) glue and cascamite.*

The glue pot (or gesso kettle) is an iron bain-marie pot with an inner reservoir of hot water. The pot is put on a fire or hotplate until the water boils, and it is then allowed to simmer gently, melting the glue ready for use. A top crust will appear and should be scraped off prior to use.

Great care should be taken not to allow the hot-water reservoir to boil dry. Should this happen, the glue will become too hot and its adhesive qualities will be lost. The remaining glue will then have to be discarded and a new batch prepared.

At the end of each day, the glue pot is taken off the heat and set aside until the next day, when it is simply reheated and the glue reused. A pot of glue could be cooled and then reheated day after day, but it is good workshop practice to make a fresh batch of animal glue every week.

Animal glue is ideal for furniture restoration because it allows a certain flexibility in the joints, it can be removed with hot water or spirit (alcohol) and it sets as soon as it has cooled. It can also be watered down to make a size for use on veneers and surfaces (see p.73) when a piece of furniture needs re-veneering.

The disadvantages of animal glue, however, are that it is affected by extremes of heat and cold and that a sharp blow to a joint will cause it to lose its adhesion. If such a break happens, the joint has to be taken apart, cleaned and reglued. Despite these disadvantages, however, no serious workshop would be without its glue pot.

Above: *Animal glues are heated prior to use in an iron bain-marie pot. The water reservoir should not be allowed to boil dry.*

PVA glue

Another frequently used glue is the more modern polyvinylacetate, or PVA (white), glue. It is bought in liquid form, is easy to use, needs no pre-application preparation and is unaffected by either extreme of temperature. The joint or two surfaces being joined must be brought under pressure when the glue (which is non-reversible) is applied.

When it is either impractical to have a glue pot simmering away all day, or when you are doing a small restoration job that simply does not warrant the time involved in preparing animal glue, versatile and simple-to-use PVA is the ideal workshop adhesive.

Cascamite

For projects needing an adhesive that will help to hold a shape or form, an ideal glue is urea-formaldehyde resin, or cascamite as it is more commonly known. This comes in a powder form and is mixed with water to a creamy paste. Once the glue has been applied, the two surfaces being joined should be brought under pressure with suitable clamps.

Cascamite is a versatile glue: its natural white colour can be disguised by adding coloured pigments to it, and some types are waterproof, which can be useful. The disadvantage, however, is that it is very brittle when set, making it totally unsuitable for joints, because just a knock could shatter the glue bond.

GILT AND STAINS

Gilding and staining are both methods of enhancing and disguising wood to give a better appearance. While stains are used in the main by the restorer to disguise repairs it should be remembered that during the 17th and 18th centuries inferior woods were often stained to give them the appearance of more exotic and expensive ones; for example pearwood was stained black to resemble the more sought after and expensive ebony.

GILT

The use of gilt to decorate and highlight furniture has been a part of furniture making for centuries. The two techniques used are those of oil and water gilding (see pp.67–69 for details), each of which gives a distinctive look. Some specialist materials and equipment are needed, but the most important ingredients that the gilder requires are patience and skill.

Gesso is a mixture of powdered chalk, rabbit-skin glue and boiled linseed melted in a gesso kettle, and it is used to build up the surface before gilding. A few layers can give a thick, even coat. It can have sand mixed in with it for a textured finish.

Bole is a mixture of clay and water that is available in red, white or blue and is used to form the next layer in the gilding process. Once this is dry, a size of alcohol, rabbit-skin glue and water is applied. The surface is now ready for the gold leaf to be laid gently in place.

The gold used in gilding has been rolled on machine rollers and then hand-hammered into leaves of varying levels of

Above: *During the 17th and 18th centuries metalware on the finest pieces was occasionally fire gilded (see p.41).*

fineness. It can be bought in a number of different grades, depending on the carat.

Agates are used to pull together joins between the leaves and for burnishing. Originally made from dog's teeth (they are also known as "dog-tooth agates"), they are now made from synthetic materials.

Right: *The tools of the gilder have remained basically the same through the centuries, although modern plastics are now replacing dog teeth.*

Water gilding

Gold leaf cannot simply be laid on to bare wood when water gilding. Bases of gesso and then bole must be applied first, and then the gilt can be laid, evened and finally distressed.

STAINS

The majority of coloured stains are either water- or spirit- (alcohol-) based, although on rare occasions a slow-drying, oil-based stain may be used. They are used to colour in repairs or to help colour out and disguise marks. Some stains can be bought in liquid form, but for the best range of tones and colours you will need to buy stains in powder form, ready to be mixed with spirit or water.

Spirit-based stains, usually mixed with methylated spirits (methyl alcohol), are quick-drying, because the spirit rapidly evaporates in air. This makes them unsuitable for use on large areas, as some areas will dry before others, causing an uneven finish. Spirit stains are usually applied after polishing. If the polish is applied on top of the stain, the spirit in the polish will dilute the stain and lighten the surface colour.

Water-based stains dry more slowly, making them suitable for large areas because they give an even finish. They are generally applied before polishing. One disadvantage, however, is that they can raise the grain, which will then need to be flattened before you can proceed any further. Both spirit and water stains can be thinned after application by adding further spirit/water.

Left: *Stains often have to be tailor-made to suit the job in hand.*

Below: *Stains can be purchased in colour powder form, which are then mixed with a suitable solvent.*

Other stains, such as coloured waxes, are not frequently used in furniture restoration. Their use is generally confined to moderating the colour of a surface slightly after it has been polished.

Stains can be applied by brush, which should be thoroughly cleaned after use with a cloth or by a dowel with some cloth wrapped around the end, known as a swab (see p.63). Alternatively, some polish can be mixed with a small amount of stain and applied not with a rubber but with a fad (see pp.64–65). This allows the whole area to be slightly tinted, and it overcomes the problem of the spirit base lightening the colour.

Mixing a spirit-based stain

1 Aways use a clean container and a flat-bladed knife or small teaspoon for mixing stains. Methylated spirits (methyl alcohol) is an ideal spirit liquid mixer.

2 Pour the required quantity of methylated spirits into the clean container. It is better to add powder to liquid rather than liquid to powder, in order to avoid unnecessary wastage. Select the correct powder required for the colour effect desired, and add a small amount at a time.

3 Mix with a clean brush. If a stronger stain tone is needed, simply add further powder. When you have finished with the stain, pour away the unused stain and clean all the utensils and the brush to ensure that the next coloured stain to be mixed is not tinted with any residue from this one.

LEATHER

One of the most commonly used writing surfaces for a desk or writing table of the 17th, 18th or 19th century was leather. The leather was often decorated with bandings applied with a hot tooling wheel. The original patinated leather, if surviving, will add great character and warmth to any piece. However, often due to its very nature, over time the leather will dry out and perish, leading to the need for a replacement to be fitted.

Since the 17th century, leather has been used as a covering on desk tops and also inset into writing surfaces. Nineteenth-century leather tops are not unusual on antique furniture, and occasionally, if it has been treated carefully, you may even find a desk or table with the original leather from the 18th century. In the majority of cases, however, cracking, tearing or wear will mean that the leather surface has to be replaced.

There are basically two types of leather to choose from: skiver (sheep leather) and hide (cow leather). Skiver is found in smaller pieces and often used on davenport tops, bureau falls (the interior of a bureau, which is used as a writing surface) and writing boxes. For larger desks and writing table tops, hide is the obvious choice due to its generally larger size. Also, as a rule of thumb, hide tends to be of better quality and more suited to quality antique furniture than skiver.

When selecting the hide or skiver for use, try to find a piece that has little or no scarring on the surface and avoid leather taken from the neck area, which tends to have stretch marks. The leather will be applied to the desk or table in its natural tan colour and will be coloured when it is in situ. Also, it is vital that the surface on to which the leather is going to be laid is level, with no cracks or splits, because these will become visible through the leather.

With the leather laid and coloured, the decorative bandings, known as tooling, must be decided upon. There are two basic types: gold tooling and blind tooling. Both are applied using a hot tooling wheel (see p.75), which embosses a pattern on to the leather surface.

The difference between the two types of banding is that the gold tooling is applied after the top has been laid and coloured, while blind tooling is embossed into the top when the leather is still wet and uncoloured, and the deep imprint is then coloured with a suitable stain.

The gold tooling effect is obtained with the tooling wheel running over a gold foil ribbon, which leaves a gold pattern. The type and style of decorative

Above: *Tooling wheels are used when heated to spitting heat. Firm and even pressure produces an excellent result.*

pattern used will often reflect the period of the piece of furniture, and a wide range of styles are available.

Above: *In "blind tooling", the tooling wheel is used without the roll of gold leaf.*

Right: *A selection of patterned borders that are available on decorative tooling wheels.*

HANDLES AND HINGES

Handles have changed greatly during the centuries in style, decoration and the materials used to make them. They were often replaced not because the originals had worn but to keep pace with the ever-changing fashions of the period. Sometimes the replacements were out of keeping with the style of the piece. Hinges were less influenced by fashion, although some were made to be more decorative to complement other furniture hardware.

THE EARLY BEGINNINGS

During medieval times, the earliest hollowed-out coffers may have had wooden peg hinges, but it was not long before the metal strap hinge began to be used. With the arrival of the plank coffer, the use of metal greatly increased. Indeed, the box chests or coffers of the 14th and 15th centuries would often have been bound with iron bands to make them stronger and to protect against splitting. By the beginning of the 15th century, hinges were becoming more elaborate with butterfly hinges, so called because they resembled butterfly wings, being used, often embossed with punched and engraved decoration.

Handles of the period tended to be ring-like in form and, like the hinges, manufactured in iron.

Left: *This 15th-century oak coffer features the stout, metal strap hinges typical of the period.*

THE 17TH CENTURY

The major changes began during the mid-to latter part of the 17th century. By this period, the business of manufacturing hinges, handles and locks (see pp.40–41) was becoming more of a specialized field. Iron was rapidly being replaced by an alloy of copper and zinc that formed the more malleable brass. Equally, the local smith was being replaced by more specialized craftsmen, from the designer and carver of the model handle, to the moulder who cast the handle and finally to the man who would chaste (carve) any pattern or design into the surface. The handle would then have the edges chamfered and be polished with a coat of lacquering to stop any tarnishing. By the mid-18th century, fire gilding (see p.41) was used on the finest of pieces.

THE 18TH CENTURY

Until the early 18th century, brass handles had been secured to the drawer with thin iron strips, or straps as they were known. From that time on, they were replaced with cast posts, or pummels, which were attached with threaded nuts to the back of the drawer.

During the late 17th century and early part of the 18th century, plate and open plate handles, which could be plain or engraved, would be made *en suite* with

Right: *This 18th-century open plate handle and matching escutcheon are typical of their period.*

Above: *Hinges could be decorative, as well as functional, but each was designed for a specific purpose.*

Left: *For the keen restorer, it is a good idea to collect antique handles and store them for future renovation projects.*

matching escutcheons to give a more consistent and balanced appearance to a piece of furniture.

During the early 18th century, the hardware would in all likelihood have been made by a local foundry. From the mid part of the century the trade became more centralized. The new foundries made handles in many different styles for the home market, but handles and other brassware were also exported, most notably for use on American and Dutch furniture.

Another material used occasionally during this period was paktong. It was an alloy of copper and zinc with nickel added to make it look like silver in appearance but at a fraction of the cost. Originally imported from the Orient, where it had been used for some time previously, it was often found on export furniture or as decorative mounts on knifeboxes.

By the latter part of the 18th century, the fashion had moved once again toward plate handles. Differing from the earlier 18th-century examples, which were cast, they were often stamped out of sheet brass, which would have had a higher copper content, making the metal more malleable. Often decorative, their centres would carry designs that, like the knob handles that followed them during the early part of the 19th century, reflected the fashion and themes of the time, with the lion mask and the Prince of Wales feather plumes both featuring heavily.

THE 19TH CENTURY

By this time, the number of foundries had greatly increased and the range of published designs had also multiplied. It is interesting to note, however, that during this period the fashion for wooden knob handles took hold. Frequently, the original brassware was removed from 18th-century furniture to be replaced with large and, most would agree, unsightly wooden examples.

Above: *18th-century swan-neck handles in various styles ranging from plain to rococo.*

Right: *A selection of 18th- and 19th-century cast knobs and pressed plate handles.*

Left: *An 18th-century card table hinge, which is distinctive because it allows the top to open then sit level with the opposite side.*

Right: *When removing antique metal care should be taken as they may be brittle and can be easily damaged.*

REPLACING HANDLES

During the centuries fashion and tastes have constantly changed, and owners often replaced perfectly serviceable hardware with something more "fashionable". So, in terms of restoration, handles are frequently replaced to bring a piece back to its original state rather than to correct any damage. To select the right kind of replacement, you will need to consult reference books and study the various styles of brassware. You might also find clues by looking for marks and shadows on the furniture, which might indicate the size and type of fitting used when the piece was first made.

Frequently, replacement handles will not have been attached to drawer and door fronts in the same way. Using the Victorian wooden door knobs as an example again, these were often attached with large screws. These holes can be disguised in a variety of ways, either by selecting plate handles which cover the damage, or by patching the holes.

Occasionally, an original handle, one of a pair or a set, may be missing. There are three main options open to you in this case: you could try and find a match from another piece of furniture or from a breaker collection; order a single replacement or a whole new set from a manufacturer specializing in period handles; or commission a copy to be made by a specialist foundry, which will use the same techniques today as were used in centuries past. Copy casting involves one of two methods: sand casting and the lost-wax process, which are explained here (see box, right).

Making copies

When the profile of the item of metalware is not too elaborate, the sand-casting process will be used. This involves placing the template piece into a two-part mould, each part of which is packed with fine casting sand. The box is then carefully separated and the template removed, leaving its profile in the sand. The two halves of the mould are then rejoined and molten brass poured in. When cool, the box is opened to reveal the newly cast metalware.

The sand-casting method, while ideal for plain metalware, is unsuitable for a more elaborate design that may have undercuts or intricate patterns. These would be lost when the piece was lifted from the sand prior to casting, and so in these cases the lost-wax technique would be used.

In the example illustrated below, one of a pair of escutcheons is missing and a copy needs to be made. Because the design of the escutcheon is very intricate and detailed, the sand-casting technique would not be suitable, whereas the lost-wax process is ideal.

First, a rubber mould is made of the escutcheon. The mould is made in two parts, each with locating pins, which allows the remaining escutcheon, which is being used as a template, to be easily removed. The empty mould is then rejoined and liquid wax poured into it. This will create a perfect replica of the escutcheon, capturing all the detail of the carving.

When the mould is cool and the wax has hardened, the wax copy is removed from the rubber mould. It is then encased in a two-part plaster mould and heated, which both hardens the plaster and melts the wax, creating a perfect hollow profile of the original escutcheon. Molten brass is then poured into the plaster mould, forcing out the liquid wax.

Left: *When the mould has cooled again, it is opened to reveal an excellent copy of the original escutcheon. Once cleaned, it can be coloured and lacquered to match the original.*

MOUNTS, CASTORS AND METALWARE

The range of mounts, castors and other metalware is vast and is influenced by the date, style and country of origin. In the past, such items were ordered from the local foundry when needed. Indeed, at times a strong indication of the piece's original maker can be gained simply by studying its original metalware. By the 18th century, the foundries were beginning to publish designs and you can often find their name stamped into a hinge, castor or lock.

Unlike today, when screws, nails and brass fittings are factory-made in their tens of thousands, the brassware and fixings of the previous centuries were all hand-made. Clout nails, which had roughly shaped heads, and hand-made screws, which had off-centre, hand-cut slots, were all works of art in their own right. It is a testament to their quality that, some 300 years after being made, they can be fixed back into their original locations ready to be used again.

As with the breaker store for wood (see p.22), or the veneer store for old surface veneers (see p.24), an equally important part of any restoration workshop is the brasswork store. Any old nails, screws or brassware that are removed from a piece of furniture are kept here for future use. While skilled foundries can make copies of period mounts, castors and galleries (small ornamental railings surrounding the top of a desk, table, etc.), there is still no substitute for the original. Each piece of bespoke brassware was designed for its particular role.

Above: *A selection of metalware dating from the 18th and 19th centuries, including mounts, castors and a section of gallery.*

Left: *A mid-18th-century Louis XV Japanese lacquer commode is richly embellished with ormolu mounts.*

Above: *A selection of 18th- and 19th-century brass castors, which, in spite of years of use, are still in working order.*

During the 18th and 19th centuries, there were two methods of treating brassware once it had been cast to prevent tarnishing: fire gilding and lacquering. Fire gilding was an expensive process usually reserved for the finest mounts, galleries and handles. The process involved mixing mercury with gold, applying it to the metalware and then heating it. The mercury would evaporate and the gold would bind to the metal. This gave a rich, bold finish, but, due to the mercury fumes that were constantly being given off, the life of the mercury gilder was a short one. The second method, lacquering, gave a similiar, if not quite as rich, appearance to fire gilding. Unfortunately, the use of

Blunting a nail

1 Knocking a large nail into a hard piece of wood, such as oak, can cause splitting. This is due to the fact that the sharp point is acting as a wedge.

2 An easy step to counter this is to blunt the point of the nail prior to use.

3 Just one or two taps with the hammer are needed to gain the desired effect.

4 With the tip now blunted, you can hammer the nail through the wood without it splitting.

abrasive solvents for cleaning over the years means that the majority of handles have lost their original finishes, but when fire-gilt and lacquered finishes are still largely intact, they should be cleaned with care (see p.55). For the most part, they need little more than an occasional wipe with a damp cloth.

Removing a nail

1 When a nail needs to be removed from a polished surface, the pliers should not touch the wood as illustrated here.

2 The pressure caused by the pliers bearing down on the wood can often cause bruising and marking to the surface polish.

3 The preferred method is to place another layer between the pliers and the polished surface. In this instance, a cabinet scraper is being used. Equally acceptable is a thin piece of wood, etc.

LOCKS AND KEYS

The range of types of key is vast, and all workshops should keep as many as possible. Often the more simple lock can be operated with a replacement key that may require little or no alteration. These antique keys can be sourced in many locations ranging from junk shops to local bric-à-brac markets. Replacement blanks, which can be cut to fit locks, are also available and can be sourced from suitable specialist suppliers.

The earliest known locks date from the Egyptian times, around 2000 BC, and the Romans also manufactured and used them. Their use continued through the ages, and by the 14th century locks were not uncommon on English furniture. Indeed, examples from the 14th and 15th centuries are to be found, with their distinctive feature of a flush face plate and sunken movement, both making sure that they could not be prised open. By the latter part of the 15th century, locks were becoming more decorative and their use increasingly widespread. In these periods, it was not only gold and valuables that required safe keeping but equally so correspondence, as a letter swearing allegiance to the wrong party could result in an untimely end.

By the late 17th century, elaborate locks were still in use, but the increasing manufacture of chests and other cabinet furniture meant that a plainer steel lock was being used, often with a simple throw mechanism. As furniture designs became more elaborate, so the need for a more tailored lock increased. Bureaux required angled face plates to mirror the fall, cupboard locks could be designed to

Left: It is important to carry a wide selection of locks and keys salvaged from breaker chests and cabinets.

throw either left or right and, where extra security was required, such as with an escritoire, three- or four-pin locks were used, which made their forcing open very difficult. On continental locks, one often finds a double throw movement, which increases the length the bolt is extended into the lock housing, thereby helping to strengthen the security of the lock.

During the 18th century, brass began to be used on the better-quality locks, although cheaper locks were still made from iron. Their manufacture began to be more elaborate, and, in 1778, a major watershed was reached when Robert Barron designed a revolutionary lever system that, unlike previous locks, which had operated on a ward system and relied on a single tumbler, operated with two tumblers, meaning that in order for the lock to throw open, the tumblers had to be lifted both back and up to a precise height. This lever system still exists in today's locks.

The lock was further developed during the 18th century by Bramah, who, in 1784, patented a system that incorporated a tube-like key with notches on the end that fitted into a lock fitted with springs, meaning that the key had to fit precisely into position in order for the lock to work. Even a slight variation would mean that the lock did not throw, and therefore a very specific key had to be used with each lock. If the key was lost, cutting a new one was a specialist task that required a trained locksmith.

It is rare that a maker would use only one specific lock or key in his furniture making, although one such exception is that of the 18th-century designer and

Right: A selection of Bramah locks with their distinctive patent pattern mark.

furniture-maker Thomas Chippendale. The use of the S key and corresponding escutcheon, while not proved to be exclusive, is widely accepted by academics and collectors alike as a mark of a piece made by Chippendale. Documented examples are to be found on pieces at Brocket Hall, Harewood House and Nostell Priory, all of which are Chippendale commissions.

While general servicing and key replacement should be able to be carried out by a competent restoration workshop, it should be remembered that some locks are very elaborate, and these more complicated examples are better dealt with by a specialist locksmith or restorer.

Above: *During the 18th and 19th centuries, a variety of locks were developed each with a specific role or task to perform.*

Servicing a lock

1 *Over the years working locks can collect all kinds of debris, such as dust, wax and even insect remains, that will eventually make the lock less efficient. A quick service is all that is needed.*

2 *Remove the lock and place it flat on a clean surface. Unscrew the retaining screws from the back plate. Take care not to misplace the original screws.*

3 *Slide the screwdriver carefully between the face and back plate and gently ease it off making sure not to damage either piece. You will now be able to see if there is any debris collected in the lock's workings.*

4 *Gently remove any debris with a soft brush. Check for any other damage while the back plate is off. If there is any rusting or parts have broken away, restoration must be carried out by a specialist locksmith.*

5 *When the lock is clean, lubricate the internal workings using a dry silicon lubricant spray. Do not use oil-based lubricants as they will quickly attract dust and cause the same problem over time.*

6 *Check that the lock works freely, then replace the back plate using the original screws. Check the lock again before placing the lock back in its original position.*

Restoration techniques

Two of the most important aspects of any piece of
antique furniture are its colour and surface
patination. Exposure to light, plus years of waxing,
causes the original wood to develop a wide range
of tones and also a surface skin, or patination,
which is highly valued by collectors and restorers.

RESTORING DAMAGED SURFACES

There are a great variety of surfaces associated with antique furniture and there are equally numerous ways in which they can be affected by excessive heat, water, moisture, grease, dirt or oxidation, to name a few. To remedy these problems each surface may need treating in a different way. Great care must be taken in the process, as a badly restored piece of furniture will not only look unsightly but be radically decreased in value.

The types of damage found on the surfaces of veneers, solid wood furniture, gilt, marble or leather fall mainly into two categories. That caused by accidental damage and that which has simply been a result of the passing of time and the action of normal wear and tear.

In some cases the damage can be corrected by little more than a light clean and a rewax, but occasionally the existing finish will have to be stripped and replaced. In the case of a gilt finish, for example, this will not be too much of a problem (the vast majority of gilded pieces have been regilded at some point). With polished surfaces, however, only the minimal amount of work should be undertaken and the work confined to the localized area of damage.

There is also the question of whether to restore a surface or leave it alone. When the damage has been caused recently, it is obvious that attention is needed. When the surface damage is old, the stain, dent or mark might have been covered with numerous generations of waxing so that it forms part of the "character" of the piece. The decision is whether to remove an unsightly mark or leave an otherwise excellent patinated surface well alone. The skilled restorer and polisher should be able to remove any localized damage successfully. The amateur restorer should not attempt this type of work on good coloured and patinated pieces. Often collectors and furniture owners alike would rather leave a mark and retain the overall integrity of a piece.

Blisters
When the glue bonding a veneered surface to its core perishes due to heat or water damage, or simply because the glue has deteriorated through age, blisters will form. The solution is either to apply hot blocks or fresh adhesive.

Water marks
Caused by either the direct or indirect action of water on a polished surface, water marks are characterized by the appearance of white patches, known as blooming. This is usually treated with new applications of polish and wax, although occasionally the surface will need to be washed back and refinished.

Spirit and water stains
Should spilled water or spirit be left to penetrate through a polished surface into the wood beneath, the result will be a black or dark stain. This can sometimes be treated with mild bleach, which will improve if not always completely remove the mark. This is, however, a specialist procedure best left to the professionals.

Dents
If dents occur on legs they can be largely ignored; if they appear on a flat, top surface they need attention. If the dent is not too deep the most common method is to try and remove it with the action of steam, which raises the grain.

Burns
The most common type of burn damage is that caused by cigarettes. A considered view should be taken to restore or not, but a burn is easier to correct on a veneered surface than a solid one. However, it is a specialist job best left to the professionals.

Scratches
Scratches are one of the most common forms of damage found on antique furniture. Light scratches that only affect the polished surface can be waxed out, while deeper ones will need to be filled and coloured out with stain.

Sunlight
The action of direct sunlight will often have an adverse effect on a polished surfaces, causing the polish to dry out and the surface to change colour. If the overall change in colour is aesthetically pleasing, it can be left; if the damage is patchy then localized areas may need to be coloured to match the rest of the surface.

Above: *Burn damage*

Above: *Scratch*

Above: *Dent*

Removing a blister

The figured walnut veneer on the top of this Regency chiffonier has blistered badly. The first solution to try is to apply a hot block in an attempt to soften the glue beneath the veneer so that it will re-adhere (see p.72). If that is not successful, the alternative is to introduce new adhesive through a cut in the veneer, but without marking the finish.

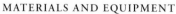

MATERIALS AND EQUIPMENT
- sharp knife
- PVA (white) glue
- clean white paper
- wooden block
- G-clamp
- rubber
- polish
- wax
- cloth (cotton rag)

1 Using a sharp knife, make small cuts in the blistered veneer to the core underneath. Follow the grain of the veneer to disguise the cuts.

2 Spread a little water on top of the cut blister; this will penetrate the incisions.

3 Spread some PVA (white) glue on top of the blister and work it in with a finger in a circular motion. The water under the veneer will draw the glue through the cuts and into the space between the veneer and core.

4 Wipe away the excess glue and place a sheet of clean white paper over the blister. Lay a hot block (heated on a hot plate or an iron, see p.72) on top and clamp it firmly in place. The paper will protect the block from the glue. Leave overnight so that the veneer can rebond with the core.

5 Remove the block and paper; carefully wash off any paper that has been stuck with excess expelled glue. If there are any minor heat marks from the hot block, charge a rubber with polish and apply a thin layer to the surface, before waxing to finish (see pp.60–61).

Above: *Once polished, no trace of the blister remains.*

Removing a water mark

The photograph below shows a common problem found on polished surfaces: a water mark caused by hot or wet items being placed directly on to a surface. In this instance, a wet vase has been placed on the table and has marked it. Fortunately, it has penetrated only the top layers of polish and not stained the actual wood. The solution is to remove the damaged polish and carefully build up the finish with fresh polish and wax so that it matches the surrounding finish. The top is quarter veneered, which means that the grain is split in four directions, so the wax must be applied in a circular motion.

MATERIALS AND EQUIPMENT

- methylated spirits (methyl alcohol)
- cloths (cotton rags)
- rubber
- polish
- wax

1 Gently wash just the affected area with a cloth (cotton rag) dipped in methylated spirits (methyl alcohol). This will remove the perished polish.

2 Charge a rubber with polish (see p.60) and apply a light layer to the washed-off area to build up the surface. Then give the whole top a rubber of polish to produce a uniform appearance (see p.61).

Above: *The water mark has now been removed without touching or altering the table's colour or patination.*

3 Allow the polish to harden, then treat the surface with a dark wax (see p.62), using circular movements.

Raising a dent

Dents and bruises are common problems with polished furniture, often caused by something being dropped on to the surface or the surface being damaged in transit. Most dents can be lifted with steam and then made invisible with polish, as shown here, but some dents are more difficult to remove. If they are not in a central position or on an otherwise unblemished surface, it is best simply to leave them alone and regard them as part of the history and character of the piece.

MATERIALS AND EQUIPMENT
- cloths (cotton rags)
- iron
- fine wire (steel) wool
- methylated spirits (methyl alcohol)
- fine-grade sandpaper
- fine brush
- spirit-based (alcohol-based) stain
- rubber
- polish
- wax

1 Place a wet cloth (cotton rag) over the dent and press the tip of a hot iron on top. This will generate steam, which will lift the bruised wood fibres. Take care to use only the tip of the iron in order to keep the steamed area as localized as possible.

2 The dent has been raised, but the steam has caused some localized damage. Use fine wire (steel) wool and methylated spirits (methyl alcohol) to wash off the areas of damaged polish.

3 The grain of the wood will have been raised by the heat. Using fine-grade sandpaper, lightly sand the repair until the wood is smooth.

4 Mix a spirit-based (alcohol-based) stain to match the colour of the table (see p.35), then carefully apply this to the restored area, disguising the raised grain. Charge a rubber with polish and seal the area by rubbing in circular motions until it is covered (see p.60–61). Leave the polish to harden.

5 Wax the affected area using fine wire wool, then wax the rest of the surface with a soft cloth until the repaired area blends in.

Right: When finished, all evidence of the dent should be removed and no trace of the restoration remain.

Disguising a scratch

A deep single scratch is not uncommon on an otherwise unmarked surface, and the aim is to try to disguise the scratch as best as possible without disturbing the rest of the polished area. If the scratch runs parallel to the grain, the task will be that much easier. If, as in this case, it runs across the grain, it will be very difficult to disguise the damage completely, although filling wax, polish and stain can produce remarkable results.

MATERIALS AND EQUIPMENT

- fine wire (steel) wool
- filling wax
- flat-bladed knife
- fine-grade sandpaper
- rubber
- polish
- spirit-based (alcohol-based) stains
- fine brush
- cloth (cotton rag)
- clear wax

Tip

Good craft stores should stock a range of coloured wax blocks for use in furniture restoration.

1 Rub the area around the scratch lightly with fine wire (steel) wool to remove the surface wax.

2 Choose a filling wax that is as close a match in colour to the table as possible. Fill the scratch with wax using a flat-bladed knife.

◁ **3** Allow the wax to harden, then gently scrape away the excess wax with a flat-bladed knife. Take great care not to mark the surface of the wood with the blade.

▷ **4** Remove the last traces of the surface filling wax with fine-grade sandpaper. Take care to avoid marking the existing polish.

5 Charge a rubber with polish and apply a layer over the scratched area to seal in the wax and blend the repair into its surroundings (see pp.60–61).

6 Mix a spirit-based (alcohol-based) stain to a colour slightly darker than the polished wax (see p.35), and apply it to the scratch with a fine brush. When the stain is dry, seal the surface with another rubber of polish.

7 Now mix a spirit-based stain to match the original surface, and apply it to the scratch with a fine brush to blend the repair into the surrounding area. Leave to dry, then seal with a rubber of polish.

8 Once the polish has dried, apply a wax coat to the whole table top. Allow the wax to dry, then buff it to a shine (see p.61).

Right: *Although the scratch has not disappeared completely, it has been disguised and looks a lot less unsightly. Most importantly, the surrounding polished area has not been altered by the repair.*

RELEATHERING A TOP

Antique writing desks with leather tops too badly damaged to be saved need to be releathered. If the desk is valuable, a top-quality piece of hide should be selected and purchased from a tannery or leather supplier. Prior to cutting it, examine it for scars, scratches and stretch marks, all of which will be emphasized when the leather is coloured and polished. Time taken at this stage will ensure that the finished result complements any other restoration work.

MATERIALS AND EQUIPMENT

- large brush
- PVA (white) glue
- leather
- "bone"
- utility knife
- cloths (cotton rags)
- leather sealant
- water-based stain
- tooling wheel
- pressurized spray gun
- cellulose lacquer
- dividers
- roll of gold leaf
- steel rule
- decorative pattern wheel
- stamp
- wax (optional)

1 To prepare the top, prise a corner of the leather free and wrap it around a long pole. Pull the leather gently away while rolling the pole towards you. Fill in any splits with strips of softwood and glue them in.

2 Apply a two-part wood filler to all cracks and knot holes with a putty knife, packing the filler in well. Leave to dry. Using fine sandpaper, smooth off the filler, making a surface the leather can stick to.

3 Spread PVA (white) glue evenly over the wood, making sure it covers the whole area, especially up to the edges. Lay the new piece of leather down on the desk top, making sure it covers the whole area.

4 With the aid of a tool known as a "bone", flatten out any blisters and uneven areas, working from the centre outward. Use the edge of the "bone" to make sure the leather is pushed into the corners (see p.36).

5 Use a sharp utility knife to cut away the excess leather, taking care that the cut is accurate and no gaps are left. Use the edge of the veneer banding as a cutting guide.

6 When the leather is dry, wipe the surface with a leather sealant, applied with a cloth (cotton rag). This will make sure that the leather dyes will give an even covering and not become blotchy.

7 Apply a water-based stain with a cloth in a circular motion and gradually build the colour to the desired intensity. Avoid the veneer banding around the edge.

8 Heat a tooling wheel to create a decorative border. Apply even pressure and, once the wheel is rolling, do not stop until you reach the end of the leather.

9 With the leather fitted, coloured and sealed, the next stage is to lacquer it. To make sure the lacquer will not mark the veneer, mask it off (wrap it) with paper.

10 Using a pressurized spray gun, apply an even coat of cellulose lacquer. If necessary, apply a second coat once the first has dried. Lacquering gives a protective layer to the leather as well as locking in the colour and stopping it bleeding out.

11 When the lacquer has dried, and the paper has been removed, decide on a decorative border. There are many styles and patterns to choose from, but it is a good idea to seek advice on what would be suitable. Use dividers to decide the best proportions.

12 Lay a roll of gold leaf in place and put a steel rule on top, then run the tooling wheel along the leaf. Keep the pressure even and ensure the wheel is at spitting heat: if too hot, it will burn through the gilt, and if too cold, the gilt will not stick to the leather.

13 Apply a more decorative pattern wheel inset inside the original single line, working freehand. Carefully peel the gold leaf away.

14 Join the corners using a stamp, which again has been heated to spitting heat. This gives a neat appearance and completes the process. The top can now be sealed with a coat of wax or another thin layer of lacquer.

15 Finally, using a utility knife, carefully lift off any excess areas of gilt and tidy up the finish. Obtaining a perfectly straight and even line, like many restoration techniques, takes many years of practice.

▷

CLEANING AND REVIVING

By its very nature and with the period of time that passes, surfaces become oxidized or coated with dust, waxes and natural greases that combine to form a surface coating. While this is desirable with wood, other materials such as metal, marble and leather may on occasion need to be cleaned or the surface revived. Different materials will require different methods, but the one common theme is to clean a little at a time to enable the desired effect to be reached and not overdone. If you are over-zealous when cleaning, the result may look rather artificial.

There are a number of steps that can be taken to help keep the need to revive or clean a surface down to a minimum. The one measure that will apply to most materials is to wax on a fairly regular basis. The wax will nourish and feed both timber and leather.

Marble, it must be remembered, is porous and to help prevent stains on the tops of tables, for example, light waxing with clear wax should be regularly applied. As well as protecting the surface, the wax will help it to develop a lustre. Regular dusting will also help to avoid the build-up of a surface coating. Dusting should be done with a dry cloth (cotton rag) – home recipes, such as the application of a harsh vinegar and water solution, should never be used. The following techniques will help to clean and revive the surfaces listed.

Cleaning marble

Over a period of years, there can be a build-up of dirt, grease and grime on marble tops. In fact, marble, like wood, often develops a warm surface patination over the years. While this can sometimes add to the colour and character, there comes a point when it will need to be cleaned. This piece of marble from an antique table is in good condition; it simply requires cleaning and sealing.

MATERIALS AND EQUIPMENT
- soda crystals
- clear wax
- cloths (cotton rags)

▷ **1** Dissolve approximately a handful of soda crystals in 4.5 litres (1 gallon) of warm water in a bowl. Use this solution to give the top a light clean, using a cloth (cotton rag) to lift off the surface dirt. Take care not to remove too much, as the natural character of the marble is part of its charm.

Tip

Marble can sometimes have an unseen fault line in it, which can crack under its own weight. When carrying a piece of marble, therefore, turn it on its side to minimize any possible risk of breakage. Remember that marble is very heavy, so enlist a helper if you have to move a large piece.

2 Using a clear wax, apply a thin coat with a cloth, rubbing with a circular motion, and allow it to harden.

3 When the wax has hardened, buff it to a soft sheen. Repeat the process until a warm patination returns to the marble.

Cleaning metal

Some metal fittings, usually brass, are gilded, while others have a lacquer coating to stop them oxidizing and the brass tarnishing. The cleaning of brass is very much a personal affair: some people may be happy to leave brass fittings completely tarnished, others may prefer to have just the highlights brightened, and others still may like to see the brass shining brightly like a soldier's buttons. If traces of the gilt or lacquer finish remain, surface grease and dirt should be removed without touching the finish underneath. In this example, two pieces of an early 19th-century cast brass moulding, known as a gallery, will be cleaned: one by a gentle method of washing with diluted soda crystals, the other using a stronger proprietary cleaning agent. The original finish on the gallery is fire-gilded.

MATERIALS AND EQUIPMENT
- soda crystals
- soft toothbrush
- de-greasant agent
- protective gloves

Tip

When cleaning mounts, mouldings, galleries or handles, it is best to remove them from the piece of furniture, if possible, to prevent any damage to the polished surface. If this is done, make a note of their location to enable them to be refitted correctly.

1 The least severe method of cleaning is to use a solution of soda crystals and water. This will gently ease off the dirt and grease without removing the finish below. Dissolve a handful of soda crystals in 4.5 litres (1 gallon) of warm water in a bowl large enough to take the metal item.

2 With a soft toothbrush, gently scrub away the residue. As this is quite a mild form of cleaning, you can leave areas of dirt in the background to give the cleaned brass a softer look. If the host piece of furniture is of good colour and patination, this is often the best and most desirable finish.

3 If you want to remove all the dirt and grease and return the gilt as closely as possible to its original state, then a strong de-greasant is recommended. Leave the brass to soak in the cleaning agent for some minutes, then scrub it with a soft toothbrush. It is advisable to wear protective gloves to prevent your skin from being stained.

Above: *The top section of gallery has been cleaned with soda crystals, giving a softer, still slightly tarnished look, while the bottom length has been cleaned with a proprietary cleaning agent, producing a brighter, harder appearance.*

Reviving leather

Leather was often used to cover writing surfaces as well as act as an upholstery material in antique furniture. Due to its nature, however, leather tends to become dry and brittle, and so usually has a shorter life than that of the piece of furniture it adorns. During the life of a piece of leather-topped furniture, therefore, the leather may have been replaced a number of times, and on occasion it may simply have been renewed because the owner wanted a colour change. Even so, a worn and textured leather surface can often enhance the character of a piece of furniture, and the surface can be revived. On this leather surface, you can see clearly where a blotter, which offered protection to the central area, has been laid. The outer, unprotected borders of the leather have become faded, worn and dry and so need to be revived.

MATERIALS AND EQUIPMENT

- brush
- clear wax
- leather-reviving cream
- rubbers
- polish
- spirit-based (alcohol-based) stain
- fine wire (steel) wool
- soft cloth (cotton rag)

1 First, brush a coat of clear wax over the whole piece of leather. This will feed and nourish the leather and provide a protective coating. Coloured wax should not be used, as it could change the overall tone. In addition to the wax, a leather-reviving cream could be applied to the piece.

2 When the wax is dry, charge a rubber with polish and apply a thin layer to the surface (see pp.60–61). This will help to seal the grain, as well as giving a protective layer in readiness for the stain. If the grain is not stained first, certain areas will absorb more stain than others, giving a blotchy look.

3 Charge a rubber with a spirit-based (alcohol-based) stain mixed to the required colour (see p.35), and apply a thin layer. This must be done in an even manner, working from the top downward. This will not disguise the worn areas totally, but it will blend them closer to the colour of the less-worn areas. When the stain is dry, apply a thin layer of polish to seal in the colour.

4 When the polish is dry, cut it back with fine wire (steel) wool with wax on it. The wax ensures that the wool does not cut back the top too much. Finally, buff to a soft sheen with a soft cloth (cotton rag).

Right: *The leather is now revived and fed. All that is necessary in future is to wax it along with the rest of the piece.*

Reviving a polished surface

General wear and tear causes most items of furniture to become discoloured and marked over time. Water marks, light scratches and stains will penetrate only the first layers of polish, allowing surfaces with this type of damage to be revived rather than completely repolished (see pp.48 and 50–51). The process of revival requires care, patience and sensitivity, but with the right application the blemishes can be erased, and the original colour and sheen will be revealed.

This top from a Georgian chest of drawers has a variety of water marks, stains and scratches. Although they are numerous, it is immediately apparent that none of the blemishes penetrates beneath the top layers of the polish, so a systematic revival of the surface is all that is required. A variety of techniques are required for this, and, when used with care, these can produce quite dramatic results, as you will see on the following page. However, as mentioned previously, any restoration work should be carried out with great care, as the idea is to attend to existing damage and not cause further problems.

MATERIALS AND EQUIPMENT
- flat-bladed knife
- fine wire (steel) wool
- linseed oil
- polish
- linen cloth
- wadding (batting)
- methylated spirits (methyl alcohol)
- fine brushes
- oxalic acid
- spirit-based (alcohol-based) stain
- rubber
- coloured wax
- soft cloths (cotton rags)

1 First remove any lumps and bumps, such as candle wax, by dragging a flat-bladed knife at a 45-degree angle across the surface. Be careful not to add any further scratches.

2 Rub the surface with fine wire (steel) wool, following the line of the grain. Failure to follow the grain could result in numerous tiny scratches, which will be difficult to remove at a later stage. Apply only very light pressure at this stage.

3 Apply linseed oil and polish to a piece of linen and rub gently in a circular motion. This will soften the top layers of polish, allowing the new colour and polish to bind to the existing surface.

4 Lightly moisten a piece of wadding (batting) with methylated spirits (methyl alcohol), and wipe it over the surface to remove any remaining traces of oil.

5 Paint over the dark inside and outside edges of the ring marks and stains using a fine brush and oxalic acid. Paint only the edges, which are always the darkest areas of ring marks and stains.

Reviving a polished surface...continued

6 Mix a spirit-based (alcohol-based) stain to match the surface colour (see p.35) and apply it with a fine brush. Try to blend the blemishes with the surrounding area rather than masking the stain with solid colour. Leave to dry.

7 Charge a rubber with polish and apply a layer of polish over the surface in even strokes (see pp.60–61). Allow to dry, then repeat until you have replaced the layers of polish removed by the linseed oil.

8 Cut back the surface by gently dusting with a piece of fine wire wool, following the grain. The idea is to even the surface and remove the glossy finish.

9 Select a wax to match the colour of the wood, and use a soft cloth (cotton rag) to apply it, rubbing with a circular motion. Leave to harden for approximately an hour.

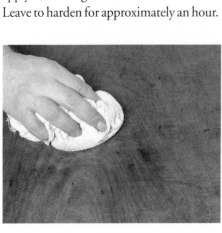

10 Buff the surface lightly with a soft cloth, following the grain. Work carefully, because the underlying polish will still be soft, and over-enthusiastic buffing will simply cause unsightly streaking.

Above: *The finished surface is now free from marks and blemishes, and the original grain, colour and patination have been revived.*

POLISHING AND COLOURING

The term "polishing" is used to describe the overall method of filling the grain and enhancing the figure of any piece of wood using shellac polish. The vast majority of polishing work today is commonly known as French polishing, which involves the use of shellac polish combined with oil – often linseed oil – and applied to the wood with a linen rubber.

Within the history of antique furniture, however, there are two very distinctive methods of finishing: varnishing using oil or spirit varnishes, and French polishing, which was introduced only in the 19th century. Both methods create distinctive appearances, and it is the effects of light, oxidation and time that make these polished and waxed surfaces so sought after by today's collectors.

The principles involved in polishing a new surface or repolishing an old surface remain the same: numerous thin layers are built up to form a combined surface. When completed, the polish should have a translucent quality that allows the colour and figure of the wood beneath to be seen. On occasion it may be necessary to tint the polish in order to adjust the final colour. This method of colouring is different from staining with spirit, water or oil, which is the process by which the actual wood tone is changed rather than simply colouring or tinting the polish.

When removing polish from a piece of furniture, it must be done a layer at a time to minimize any damage to the colour and surface of the piece. When the damaged areas have been carefully lifted, further polish can again be applied, a layer at a time, until the required surface appearance is obtained. If too much polish is applied the surface will have a treacle-like appearance; if too little polish is used the grain in the wood will look open and "hungry", resulting in a blotchy effect once the surface has been waxed.

French polishing

Prior to the early 19th century the methods of finishing furniture were mainly the application of varnishes or oils such as linseed and various wax compounds. These were usually applied, often by brush or cloth (cotton rag), after the grain had been sealed with ground brick dust or pumice powder. They served to protect the wood and could be burnished to a soft lustre finish.

In 1820 a new practice, imported from France, came to favour. It was the use of shellac, which comes from the shells of the lac beetle. The shellac, which was dissolved in spirit, was applied layer by layer, giving a hard, glossy finish. Over the years, and with the application of wax, the hard, glossy surfaces mellow, and depending on the style and period of the piece, the surface finish can range from hard and glossy to a soft, almost matt appearance.

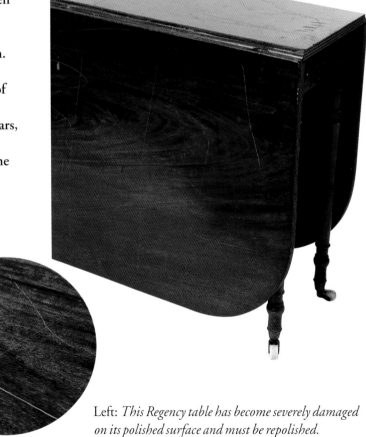

MATERIALS AND EQUIPMENT
- wadding (batting)
- linen
- polish
- fine wire (steel) wool
- methylated spirits (methyl alcohol)
- soft cloth (cotton rag)
- shellac
- linseed oil
- clear beeswax

Left: *This Regency table has become severely damaged on its polished surface and must be repolished.*

MAKING AND CHARGING A RUBBER

A rubber is an essential tool for applying a French polish finish and is easy to make. All you need is some wadding (batting) or plain unmedicated cotton wool and a square of linen or similar lint-free cloth. The rubber acts in the same manner as a sponge, absorbing a quantity of the polish (known as charging), which is squeezed out on to the surface being polished when you apply pressure to it. A rubber can also be used to apply a stain to wood.

▷ **1** Lay a 15cm/6in long piece of wadding (batting) on the centre of a piece of linen the size of a large handkerchief.

2 Fold the ends of the linen inward and grasp them in the centre of your palm.

3 With all the outer edges gathered together, twist the ends of the linen to form a tail.

4 The rubber is complete when the tail is completely twisted. For a smaller, more intricate, polishing job, make a smaller rubber to suit.

◁ **5** To charge the rubber, open out the linen to expose the wadding, then pour a small amount of polish on to the wadding. With practice, you will be able to judge the correct quantity. Note that if the rubber is too dry it will not run smoothly over the surface; if it is too wet it will simply lay the polish on the surface.

▷ **6** Refold the linen around the wadding. Squeeze the tail to apply pressure to the wadding, to force the polish through the linen. The more you tighten the tail, the more polish will emerge. After polishing, you can store the rubber for another day.

APPLYING THE POLISH

If the damage to a surface is extensive, it will have to be stripped back with methylated spirits (methyl alcohol) before repolishing, as shown here. New wood is polished in much the same way, except that the grain is first filled with pumice and polish, then sanded flat with very fine or broken down sandpaper.

Once the rubber has been charged, the polish can be applied. This process takes time, and the finish must be left overnight for the polish to harden before it can be buffed to a high sheen or cut back to produce a matt finish.

Tip

When polishing with a rubber (step 3) the idea is to "body up" or fill the grain. This is done by first applying the polish in straight continuous strokes along the grain (below top). The polish is then applied in circular motions (below centre) and finally with wider figure of eight movements (below bottom).

1 Remove the old polish and wax surface with fine wire (steel) wool and methylated spirits (methyl alcohol).

2 Once the old polish and wax have been removed, wash off the surface with a soft cloth (cotton rag) and methylated spirits.

3 Polish the surface using a rubber and shellac (see Tip). Linseed oil can be dripped on to the surface to help lubricate the rubber. This technique, known as "bodying up", fills the grain. Leave for at least 24 hours to harden.

4 When the polish has hardened, cut it back lightly using fine wire wool and working in the direction of the grain. Use light strokes to remove any raised nibs of polish. This also produces a higher gloss finish.

5 Finally, apply a coat of wax. Use light strokes as the polished surface will still be delicate. Allow to stand for a week before use to allow the polish to fully harden.

Right: *When polished, the scratches become invisible and the table has an even, soft sheen that should last for years.*

Waxing

All antique furniture will require waxing during its lifetime. Waxing feeds, protects and nourishes the wood. It is the combination of waxes with natural grease and oxidation that forms the surface patination that is so desirable. Over the generations, various types of wax have been used, with workshops producing their own secret recipes.

One of the most common misconceptions is that the more frequently a piece is waxed. the fuller the finish will be. Over-waxing will result in smeary surfaces, since wax softens wax.

The only remedy for this is to remove all the wax and begin afresh. It is far better to wax at sensible intervals and apply only a very thin layer. Use only natural wax-based products.

MATERIALS AND EQUIPMENT	
• clear wax	• soft cloths (cotton rags)
• soft brush	• brush

WAXING A FLAT SURFACE

1 Apply a thin layer of wax using a soft cloth (cotton rag) impregnated with the chosen wax. Never apply too thick a layer, as this will simply make the rubbing up more difficult and time consuming.

2 Even out the wax using a soft brush. Take care not to mark the surface and make sure you work along the direction of the grain. Use long, steady strokes, working from one side of the surface to the other.

3 Allow the wax to harden for a few minutes, then buff the surface vigorously with a soft cloth, working in the direction of the grain. Finally, use a clean cloth to give the surface a final burnish.

WAXING A CARVED SURFACE

1 Due to the nature of the hollows and relief, it is better to apply a thin coat of wax with a soft brush, making sure that it is neither too hard nor too soft.

2 Allow the wax to harden for a few minutes, then gently burnish the carving with a soft brush. This will remove any surplus wax and even out what remains.

3 Finally, buff the highlights using a soft cloth (cotton rag). Mutton cloth, which is available from most trade suppliers, is ideal for this role.

Staining

Paints and varnishes adhere to the surface of the wood, but stains penetrate it, changing its colour permanently. For this reason, stains are favoured by the restorer. They can enrich dull-looking wood or change the colour of new wood so that it blends in with the rest of the piece of furniture. This bureau has had a new piece of wood added to it that must be stained and polished so that it matches the rest of the piece.

MATERIALS AND EQUIPMENT
- spirit-based (alcohol-based) stain
- cloth (cotton rag)
- wooden dowel
- fine brush
- rubbers
- polish
- methylated spirits (methyl alcohol)
- soft brush
- wa•

Tip

Spirit-based (alcohol-based) stains, thinned with methylated spirits (methyl alcohol), are the best stains to use, because they dry very quickly. However, they are harder to obtain and more difficult to use. This is because they can leave obvious overlap marks. Solvent- and water-based stains are available ready mixed and are easier to apply.

1 Use a spirit-based (alcohol-based) stain mixed to match the colour of the furniture. For a small area like this, wrap a piece of cloth (cotton rag) around one end of a dowel and use this to apply the stain to the new piece of wood. If staining a large area, use a brush to apply the stain. Continue until the colour is even, then leave to dry.

2 Check again that the stain is even. If necessary, add another layer, or draw in the grain with a fine brush (see p.66). When you are satisfied with the colour of the dried stain, charge a rubber with polish and apply a layer to the stain, and also to the rest of the bureau to blend in the stained area (see pp.60–61). Allow the polish to dry.

3 Cut back the polish with a rubber charged with a little methylated spirits (methyl alcohol). The new wood should now be indistinguishable from the old.

4 Use a soft brush to apply a thin coat of wax to the new wood, and the rest of the piece of furniture, to give a soft, even sheen. Leave to dry.

Above: *Now stained and polished, the new wood blends seamlessly with the old.*

Modifying the colour

The room for which a table was initially commissioned will often not be the one in which it spends the majority of its life, and in the case of larger tables not all the original leaves will be used. An extra leaf may well be stored under a bed or in a cupboard, where it will keep its natural colour while the rest of the table will fade and mellow in colour. When the time comes to set the table up to its full size, it will be necessary to modify the colour and tone of the unused leaf to match the rest of the table.

This mahogany table shows how the two ends have been used together for most of the time – they have a warm, even colour and wax patination – but the middle leaf has had almost no use and remains much darker than the other leaves. The technique for lightening the darker section requires that the

original polished finish be removed with a weak solution of paint stripper, after which the wood can be made paler with a solution of oxalic acid or bleach.

MATERIALS AND EQUIPMENT
- protective gloves
- weak paint stripper
- brush
- flat-bladed knife
- coarse wire (steel) wool
- cloths (cotton rags)
- methylated spirits (methyl alcohol)
- oxalic acid
- mutton cloth
- bleach
- acetic acid
- dowel
- rubber
- polish
- spirit- (alcohol-) based stain
- fine wire wool
- dark wax

1 Apply a weak solution of paint stripper with a brush in 30cm/12in squares. The reason for using a weak stripper is that it is required to remove only the top layers of polish and wax. Under no circumstance should it be allowed to bite into the wood.

2 Once the stripper has been applied, the polish will begin to glaze and congeal. At this point, use a flat-bladed knife to gently scrape away the dissolved polish and wax, taking great care not to mark the wood.

3 With coarse wire (steel) wool, remove any residue of polish and wax. The wire wool should simply be slid over the surface and not applied with any pressure, as this would cause unnecessary and unsightly damage.

4 Use a clean cloth (cotton rag) to wipe methylated spirits (methyl alcohol) over the table top. This will neutralize any residue of the stripper. Make sure that you apply it evenly across the whole surface.

5 Having removed all the polish and wax, you now need to colour the wood to match the desired shade. The first method to try is to mix one part oxalic acid with ten parts hot water and apply the mixture with a pad of mutton cloth.

6 In this case, the oxalic acid was too weak to lighten the leaf to the desired tone, so you will need to try another method, this time using bleach.

7 To lighten the table further, apply bleach with a cloth. Wear gloves to protect your skin. Initially, treat the wood with a solution of one part bleach to three parts water. If this is unsuccessful, treat the wood with one part bleach to one part water.

8 When completed, neutralize the bleach by applying acetic acid using a cloth or a dowel with cloth wrapped around the end. The leaf is now ready to be polished and coloured to match the rest of the table.

9 Lay the bleached leaf beside one of the end leaves to see if the correct tone and colour cast have been obtained. Charge a rubber with polish and apply a thin layer to the lightened leaf to indicate its final colour.

10 If the colour and tone need further adjustment, mix a spirit-based (alcohol-based) stain to the colour required (see p.35) and apply it to the whole leaf or just localized areas, using a cloth.

Left: After applying the coloured stain, you will need to add several rubbers of polish (see pp.60–61). Allow each layer of polish to sink in before applying the next. It is advisable to allow the last layer of polish to settle for a couple of days to ensure that the grain has been filled completely. After the top has hardened fully, cut it back lightly with fine wire wool, then apply a thin coat of dark wax using a soft cloth (see p.61). When cutting back and waxing, make sure that you work in the direction of the grain.

Graining

During the late 18th and early 19th centuries, rosewood was imported from India, South America and the West Indies for use in the manufacture of furniture. It was an expensive wood, and so only the finest pieces of furniture were made from solid rosewood; other pieces were made from beech, which was a hard-grained, easily workable, cheap native wood. The beech was "grained" with a paint finish to give the appearance of rosewood. Over time, the areas of graining wear away, revealing the beech underneath, as has happened with this Regency chair. In this case, it is necessary to simulate the rosewood graining while also giving it a patinated, antique look. The techniques for distressing are varied and include using smooth stones, fine wire (steel) wool and homemade tools. These should be practised and perfected before use.

MATERIALS AND EQUIPMENT
- light brown spirit-based (alcohol-based) stain
- fine brushes
- screwdriver
- rubber
- polish
- dark brown spirit-based stain
- wax
- cloth (cotton rag)

Above: *An area of the graining has worn away on the chair leg to reveal the beech wood underneath.*

1 Apply a base coat of a light brown stain mixed to match the base colour of the rest of the chair (see p.63). Leave to dry. Charge a rubber with polish and apply a thin layer.

2 Apply a dark brown stain mixed to match the grain of the simulated rosewood, using a fine brush to replicate the pattern. If no residue of graining is left, use a piece of patinated rosewood veneer as a pattern.

3 When the graining is dry, distress the graining effect using a screwdriver, if necessary, to match the original. Give it another rubber of polish to seal in the effect, then wax the chair using a cloth.

Above: *The grained beech chair, on the right of the picture, now looks very similar to the solid rosewood chair on the left. Both these chairs are dining chairs, made c.1810.*

Gilding

Water gilding requires great patience and an extremely delicate touch. Leaves of hand-beaten gold, beaten to a thickness of 0.025mm (0.001in) thick, are expensive, so it is wise to practise with metal leaf, which is much cheaper, until you are confident.

This 18th-century carved wood and gilt frame had been weakened by worm, which led to it becoming detached from its wire hooks and falling to the floor, causing considerable damage. Fortunately, most of the pieces had been kept together.

MATERIALS AND EQUIPMENT

- animal glue
- two-part epoxy resin
- wood carving tools
- gesso and gesso kettle
- soft brushes
- fine-grade sandpaper
- bole
- size
- fine brush
- gold leaf
- suede pad
- blunt knife
- gilder's fitch or good-quality artist's brush
- agate

1 Place the frame on a flat surface and glue the separate parts together. Leave to dry.

2 Fill the missing areas with two-part epoxy resin. This useful substance offers strength as well as malleability. It will bond easily with the damaged parts.

3 After the resin has hardened, carve it to follow the line of the existing frame using normal wood carving tools.

4 Heat a quantity of gesso in a gesso kettle to the consistency of double (heavy) cream. Apply it to the frame with a soft brush. Continue applying layers until you obtain the desired thickness. Leave to dry. ▷

Gilding...continued

5 Shape the gesso with carving tools and cut in any detailing. It is always the gesso that is carved, rather than the wood, which is why many intricate mirrors with carved decoration appear quite ordinary when stripped back to the wood prior to regilding.

6 Give the gesso the lightest of sandings with very fine-grade sandpaper. The purpose of this is simply to remove any raised nibs and to smooth the sweeping curves.

◁ **7** Paint a thin layer of bole on to the gesso. Red bole is being used here to match the original bole colour of the mirror. Following the method used with the gesso, warm the bole and apply it with a soft dry brush. When dry, smooth lightly with fine-grade sandpaper.

▷ **8** Place a sheet of gold leaf on a suede pad edged with stiff card for protection, and peel off the backing. Take care when handling gold leaf, since even the lightest of draughts will blow it out of line.

9 Cut the gold leaf into a number of small sections with a flat-bladed, blunt knife; only the lightest of pressures is required. Note how the unused scraps (offcuts) of gold leaf are left at the back of the pad to be used for faulting (filling in any small areas).

10 Apply a coating of size to the frame with a fine brush. Apply it to small areas at a time, followed by the immediate application of the pre-cut gold leaf.

11 The leaf is so light that it can prove difficult to handle. One of the best techniques is simply to use static electricity. Rub a clean gilder's fitch or artist's brush against your skin to build up a little static.

12 With the fitch or brush charged, simply touch the bristles to the gold leaf to lift it from the pad and place it on the frame.

13 Lay the leaf on the sized area. The size will pull it down on to the various contours. Repeat this process until all the areas of bole have been covered. This requires patience, and rushing will affect the final finish.

◁ **14** After gilding a significant area, dust over with a large soft brush, called a mop. This will remove any loose and excess gilt, exposing any uncovered areas. Use the gilt scraps saved for faulting to fill these gaps.

▷ **15** With the frame now fully gilded, use an agate to burnish the surface. This will give an even finish and tone to the gilt throughout. Take care not to remove the delicate gilt surface.

Oil gilding

Oil gilding is a much simpler process than water gilding. After the gesso has been applied, the area to be gilded is painted with a special oil gilt size. The gold leaf is then laid directly from the sheet, held into place by its own backing. Oil gilding can even be used straight on to a wood surface. Unlike water gilding, the gilded surface is not burnished after application, so the carat of leaf used dictates the finish.

Above: The fully restored frame is now ready to be fitted with its mirror plate. All evidence of the extensive damage has now been removed.

VENEERING

During the history of furniture making, the introduction of certain new techniques has radically altered the design and form of furniture. The skill of veneering, where thin layers of wood are laid on top of a different base wood, was introduced in the 17th century and this resulted in furniture taking on a much more flamboyant appearance. Woods that had previously been used in the solid could now be hand cut into thin sheets and laid to display the distinctive patterns of the wood, thereby greatly enhancing the look of furniture.

Highly decorative burrs and pollards, which had been too unstable to use in the solid, could now be cut and laid on to stable cores. It was indeed a giant step forward in the history of furniture construction.

The use of veneer in furniture construction became more popular during the latter part of the 17th century and the 18th century; prior to this it was used sparingly in decoration but more in a marquetry or parquetry form. Veneer was preferred over the solid during this period as it enabled a more decorative appearance to be achieved. For this reason it is common to find quarter-veneered tops or bookmatch drawer fronts from this period. Indeed, during the latter part of the 18th century, it was usual to find expensive decorative veneer such as mahogany laid on top of an equally expensive, but plainer, mahogany core.

This reflects the philosophy of this time when the use of veneer was more about aesthetics than economy. The quality of an individual's furniture was also seen to reflect the wealth of its owner and their position in society. However, by the 19th century, with the ability to cut wood mechanically, combined with the increasing demand for furniture by the merchant classes, the use of veneer enabled cheaper furniture to be made that could still be covered by the fashionable and expensive imported woods such as mahogany and satinwood.

Above: *A selection of old surface veneers.*

Above: *A late 17th-century bureau veneered in walnut rather than made from the solid wood.*

Above: *A George III linen press veneered in figured mahogany throughout.*

Above: *A Regency period drawer front veneered with figured rosewood and burr amboyna, and inlaid with brass decoration.*

Above: *A walnut bookmatch veneered end.*

Removing veneer

On the whole, veneer does not need to be removed. Either it will be loose, in which case it can be heated and clamped back into position (see p.72) or it will be missing. In some instances, however, a previous repair may have to be removed because it was not done professionally. In the example here, the veneer patch is rectangular and can easily be seen. Had it been cut to follow the pattern of the grain, it would have blended in with the rest of the piece more successfully. The old piece of veneer must be removed completely before the new patch can be cut in.

MATERIALS AND EQUIPMENT
- fine wire (steel) wool
- methylated spirits (methyl alcohol)
- metal rule
- utility knife
- masking tape
- chisel
- iron
- veneer
- PVA (white) glue
- clamping blocks
- G-clamps
- rubber
- polish

1 Wipe over the veneer patch with fine wire (steel) wool soaked in methylated spirits (methyl alcohol) until the polish comes off the patch. This allows you to see exactly where the patch meets the rest of the veneer.

2 Use a metal rule and a utility knife to score along the edges of the patch, making sure you cut all the way through the veneer.

3 Push a chisel under the veneer patch and place a hot iron on top. Lift and remove the veneer patch in sections, continuing until it is all gone. Be careful not to put the iron on any of the original veneer.

◁ **4** Select a veneer that has appropriate graining and pattern, and cut out a piece, following the pattern, that is slightly larger than the area to be patched.

▷ **5** Place the new veneer over the area to be patched and use a utility knife to cut a new patch to fit the shape. Glue it in place with PVA (white) glue, apply clamping blocks and leave to dry. Stain and colour the veneer patch to blend with the surrounding wood (see p.63). Some graining may need to be added, too (see p.66). Finally, polish the patched area (see pp.60–61) and wax to finish (see p.62).

Laying veneer sheets

Small areas of veneer are simple to glue and clamp into place; the difficulty is in selecting the correct veneer. Larger areas of veneer cannot be clamped; instead, they are sealed with a different glue and a veneer hammer, which is a rather complicated procedure. To veneer curved surfaces, a counter-core must be made, which allows the clamps to exert even pressure on the drying veneer. Corners and edges of veneer will often be missing or split after years of use.

MATERIALS AND EQUIPMENT
- MDF (medium-density fiberboard)
- iron
- screwdriver
- paper
- clamping block
- G-clamps
- utility knife
- veneer
- PVA (white) glue
- ebony stringing
- masking tape
- rubber
- polish

LAYING SMALL AREAS OF VENEER

This bracket clock is veneered in Cuban mahogany. The veneer is loose, and parts of the veneer and the ebony stringing have been broken off and lost. It is not necessary to re-veneer the loose areas of veneer as they can simply be rebonded to the core.

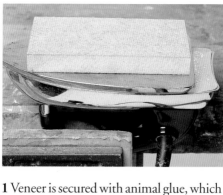

1 Veneer is secured with animal glue, which means that heat and pressure can often be enough to rebind the veneer. Heat a piece of MDF (medium-density fiberboard) on an iron for approximately 5 minutes.

◁ **2** Remove the base section, taking care not to lose the screws. Place a piece of paper on the upper side of the veneer, and a clamping block below, to prevent damaging the carcass. Clamp the hot MDF into place, then leave until cool.

▷ **3** Cut a piece of veneer slightly larger than the missing piece. Cut the damaged area to the size of the new piece, then glue the new veneer in place. Clamp it until the glue dries, using a clamping block.

◁ **4** Select a new length of ebony stringing (see p.79). Cut this to size, glue it in place and secure with masking tape. (Note that there is no need to soak the stringing because it does not have to be shaped.) Reattach the base. Charge a rubber with polish and apply a thin layer over the whole carcass (see pp.60–61).

Right: *A good match for the original veneer was found, making the repair to this clock completely invisible.*

LAYING LARGE AREAS OF VENEER

There is little call to lay new veneer in most antique furniture restoration, but in some circumstances, such as extreme fire or water damage or if large areas of veneer are missing, this may be needed. The tools used are almost identical to those utilized by cabinet-makers over the past 200 years.

MATERIALS AND EQUIPMENT

- fine wood filler
- putty knife
- smooth toothing plane
- short, thick brush
- animal glue
- newspaper
- veneer
- veneer hammer
- cloth (cotton rag)
- flat piece of wood
- utility knife
- steel straightedge
- cabinet scraper
- medium fine-, fine- and very fine-grade sandpaper
- sanding block

◁ **1** First, prepare the base wood by filling any splits or dents with a fine wood filler. If these are not filled, they will show through the veneer when it is laid.

▷ **2** When the filler has hardened, level it using a smooth toothing plane. This will also key the surface for the veneer and adhesive.

3 Brush a size made of animal glue and hot water over the surface of the carcass. This will fill the grain and ensure that when the animal glue is applied prior to veneering, it will produce an even layer. Failure to do so can result in blisters in the veneer. Protect the rest of the carcass with newspaper.

4 Veneering half the surface at a time enables you to work while the glue is still malleable. Coat half the surface liberally with animal glue, then lay the veneer and use a veneer hammer with a firm pressure to expel all the excess glue. Dip the hammer into a mixture of glue and hot water to help it glide easily.

5 When half the surface is covered, wash off the surface of the veneer with a hot, wet cloth (cotton rag) to remove any traces of animal glue.

▷

Laying large areas of veneer...continued

6 Trim the excess veneer by placing a flat piece of wood against the edge and scoring around the shape of the carcass with a utility knife. The wood will prevent the veneer from splitting.

7 Repeat the veneering process on the other half. To obtain a perfect join, overlap the first piece of veneer with the second. Lay a steel straightedge over both pieces and cut through them with a utility knife.

8 Lift away the trimmed strips from both sections of veneer, leaving a perfect join. Run the veneer hammer along this join to make sure the edges lie flat. Leave to dry overnight.

9 When the glue is dry, go over the newly veneered section with a cabinet scraper. This will level the veneer and flatten the grain, which will have become raised with the application of hot water.

10 Finally, use three grades of sandpaper (graduating all the time to the finest grade) wrapped around a sanding block to remove all scraper marks and prepare the veneer for polishing.

LAYING CURVED VENEER

On occasion, you may need to make or replace a missing veneered part for a piece of furniture that is shaped. For example, a moulding may have lost its veneer, or, as in this case, a piece of furniture has lost its cornice, so a replacement cornice (known as a core) needs to be made and then veneered to match.

MATERIALS AND EQUIPMENT
- pine or mahogany
- band saw
- moulding plane
- veneer
- brush
- animal glue
- G-clamps
- utility knife
- curved cabinet scraper
- fine-grade sandpaper

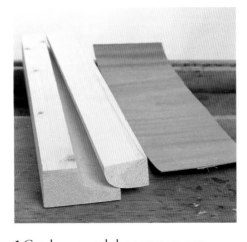

1 Cut the core and also a counter-core, which follows the internal curve of the core or original moulding, out of pine or mahogany using a band saw or spoke shave. Shape both pieces with a moulding plane. Select a length of veneer that is wider than the core or moulding.

2 To make the veneer malleable so that it does not crack or split when applied, soak it in water until pliable. An old tin bathtub is often best for such a task, as it allows veneers of a good length to be soaked. Change the water if you plan to use different veneers, to prevent staining.

3 Remove the veneer from the bath and, while it is still wet and pliable, brush animal glue evenly over the core or moulding, and press the veneer firmly on to it.

4 Place the counter-core on top of the veneer and clamp it tightly. Make sure that an even pressure is applied throughout to ensure that no blisters result. Leave the veneer to dry overnight.

5 When the glue is dry, remove all but one of the clamps, but leave the counter-core in place while you trim off the excess veneer with a utility knife. The remaining clamp acts as a useful handle.

◁ **6** Remove the final clamp and the counter-core. Clean up the veneer with a curved cabinet scraper, applying an even pressure. The idea is to remove fine shavings and not to tear the grain.

▷ **7** Go over the veneer with fine-grade sandpaper. A section cut from the counter-core, which will fit into the shape of the moulding or core, makes a suitable sanding block for this purpose.

RESTORING EDGES AND INLAYS

Tops of tables, desks and cabinets are subject to more general wear and tear than practically any other areas of furniture. Scratches, dents and stains are commonplace (see pp.57–58). Other frequent problems that occur with tops are warping, splitting and damaged decorative edges, banding and stringing. Marquetry and parquetry are also vulnerable to damage. By using the correct restoration techniques, however, it is possible to make good all of these defects and to bring a damaged edge or inlay back to the prime condition it was in when the piece was made.

Restoring a damaged edge

This Cuban mahogany Georgian tripod table is missing a section of its decorative edge. A new piece of wood needs to be cut, glued in place and shaped to fit, before being stained and polished to match the table top. This technique can be used on all moulded edges, including pie-crust tops.

MATERIALS AND EQUIPMENT
- screwdriver
- mahogany
- jigsaw (saber saw)
- tenon saw
- chisel
- PVA (white) glue
- spring clip
- plane
- carving tool
- spokeshave
- fine-grade sandpaper
- brush
- stain
- rubber
- polish

◁ **1** Remove the table top from the frame by undoing all the screws. Turn the table top upside down and lay it on a protected surface. Put a piece of mahogany, slightly thicker than the decorative edging, underneath the top, and draw around the edge with a pencil. Slide the mahogany farther out by an amount slightly greater than the width of the decorative edging, and draw another curved line.

2 Cut the mahogany along the pencil lines using a jigsaw (saber saw), then turn the table top right side up again. Cut through the damaged edging on either side of the missing area with a tenon saw.

3 Remove the damaged wood underneath the missing edging with a chisel. Continue working until you have a flat, level surface.

4 Check that the piece of mahogany fits in the allotted space. Apply PVA (white) glue and secure it with a spring clip. Leave to dry, then remove the spring clip.

5 Plane the mahogany down until it is level with the rest of the edging. Make small strokes to avoid damaging the table top.

6 The inner ledge on the table must be shaped with a suitable carving tool. Again, avoid damaging the polished mahogany.

7 Use a spokeshave to shape the curve along the edge of the top. It is easier to obtain a more delicate shape with a spokeshave than a plane.

8 Smooth the top of the restored area with fine-grade sandpaper. Fold a small piece of the sandpaper in half and hold it with your thumb and forefinger for accuracy.

Above: *Once the detailed shape of the edging has been formed with sandpaper, stain (see p.75) and polish (see pp.60–61) the repaired edging so that it is invisible.*

Replacing bandings

Decorative veneer inlays situated around the edges of tables, chests and cabinets are known as bandings. They are usually cut from the same veneer as the main body veneer, but across, rather than along, the grain to distinguish them from the body veneer. Their position makes bandings vulnerable to knocks, and they are often the first piece of veneer to break off. This table has lost part of its banding.

MATERIALS AND EQUIPMENT

- veneer
- utility knife
- dividers
- PVA (white) glue
- clamping blocks
- G-clamps
- chisel
- fine-grade sandpaper
- spirit-based (alcohol-based) stain
- cloth (cotton rag)
- wooden dowel
- rubber
- polish

1 Cut out the chosen veneer with a utility knife into lengths of approximately 10cm/4in. If the table is curved, place a length of veneer under the edge or, in this case, the flap, and draw around the edge.

2 Scratch the width of the missing banding on to the veneer, using a pair of dividers. Remember to mark across, rather than along, the grain. Cut out the banding.

3 Make sure that the area to be veneered is clean before applying a thin layer of PVA (white) glue. Lay one piece of veneer on the glue and press it down. Clamp using G-clamps and blocks and leave for a few hours.

4 When the glue is dry and the bond secure, remove the clamps and blocks and level the veneer with a chisel. Take care not to damage the main body of veneer.

5 Repeat with the remaining veneer, then smooth with fine-grade sandpaper. The new banding should sit flush with the old and follow the curve of the table exactly.

Above: *Once it has been stained and polished (see p.63 and pp.60–61), the new banding should blend seamlessly with the old.*

Replacing stringings

Very thin, string-like pieces of veneer, usually cut from boxwood, are also used as decorative veneer inlays. Stringings are often situated next to bandings, and are just as likely to be knocked, as was the case with this table, which has lost part of its stringing. For this project the stringing is soaked and applied wet as it needs to be malleable in order to bend around the curved shape of the table.

MATERIALS AND EQUIPMENT
- utility knife
- stringing
- PVA (white) glue
- masking tape
- chisel
- fine-grade sandpaper
- spirit-based (alcohol-based) stain
- cloth (cotton rag)
- wooden dowel
- rubber
- polish

1 Using a utility knife, cut a length of stringing from a piece that matches the original in dimension and colour. Soak the stringing in some hot water to make it more malleable.

2 While the stringing is still wet, glue it in place with PVA (white) glue. Tape it down with masking tape and leave to dry.

3 When the stringing is dry, level the top and sides with a chisel. Take care not to damage the existing veneer.

4 Smooth the stringing with fine-grade sandpaper. Continue until the edges are blunted and the veneer is level.

Left: *Once stained and polished (see p.63 and pp.60–61), the new stringing is indistinguishable from the old.*

Marquetry repairs

Intricate veneer inlay in the shape of flowers, leaves and other natural objects is known as marquetry. This table is Dutch in origin and was made c.1740. It is veneered in walnut with marquetry panels of box, sycamore and walnut laid on to an oak core. It is of good colour and patination, but there has been some shrinkage to the oak carcass, which in turn has damaged the marquetry panels. Closer inspection reveals that previous losses of veneer and marquetry have been disguised with coloured filler.

MATERIALS AND EQUIPMENT
- fine wire (steel) wool
- small chisel
- tracing paper
- veneer
- fret saw
- PVA (white) glue
- masking tape
- fine brush
- spirit-based (alcohol-based) stain
- rubber
- polish

1 First, expose the old coloured-out parts by rubbing off the entire surface colour from the filler with fine wire (steel) wool.

2 The areas of missing marquetry will now be visible. Remove the old filler with a small chisel, taking care not to dig into the core.

3 Determine the style and shape of the missing marquetry by looking for corresponding areas of marquetry that are undamaged. Trace their shapes carefully.

4 Offer up the tracings to the areas of missing marquetry and carefully position the copied patterns to ascertain which designs need to be cut.

5 Cut the veneer with great care, using a fret saw. Once each piece is cut, stick it in place with PVA (white) glue, then tape it into position and leave to dry.

Above: *Once all the missing pieces of veneer have been replaced, the area needs to be stained and polished (see p.63 and pp.60–61). The table should then look as it did in 1740.*

Parquetry repairs

Intricate veneer inlay in geometric shapes, such as diamonds and squares, is known as parquetry. It often utilizes differently coloured and grained veneer to give a three-dimensional effect. Some areas of the parquetry on this cabinet have worn away and must be replaced.

MATERIALS AND EQUIPMENT

- veneer
- sliding bevel gauge
- utility knife
- small chisel
- PVA (white) glue
- masking tape
- small blade
- spirit-based (alcohol-based) stain
- cloth (cotton rag)
- wooden dowel
- rubber
- polish

1 Select a replacement veneer that has a similar grain and can be polished to the same colour as the existing veneer.

2 Cut the veneer to size using a sliding bevel gauge and a utility knife. This will make sure that the angles are correct so that you can achieve an exact fit.

3 Remove the damaged veneer with a small chisel, making sure that you remove complete shapes from damaged areas. Do not touch the surrounding veneer.

4 Glue the new pieces in place with PVA (white) glue and tape them down with masking tape. When the glue is dry, scrape the new pieces with a small blade until they lie flush with the other pieces.

Left: *Careful choice of veneer needs to be followed by expertly applied stain and polish (see p.63 and pp.60–61) to ensure that the restored diamond shapes echo the distinctive grain and patina of the original parquetry.*

PROJECT: ROSEWOOD POLE SCREENS

Pole screens began to appear at the beginning of the 18th century. They were designed to protect women's faces from the heat of the fire. With the advent of coal-fired boilers in the late 19th century, their manufacture all but ceased.

These items of furniture make interesting decorative pieces in their own right, however, and are well worth restoring. They are likely to have suffered from a variety of ills.

ASSESSING THE PROJECT

These William IV rosewood pole screens have several areas of damaged veneer and wood that need to be repaired or replaced. Most importantly, both frames for the screens are missing, so these will have to be built from scratch. Research into the history of the pieces shows that they ought to have oval frames, and the owner has chosen some suitable material to fit.

The base and pole
- loose veneer
- missing veneer
- broken screw thread

The frame
- missing frame

Repairing the base and pole

Damp had caused the glue joining the veneer to the core to perish, allowing the veneer to become detached and, in some areas, to break off completely. The glue joining the main body of the feet to the scrolling top sections had also perished, and while some of the pieces could simply be reglued, others were missing and would have to be recarved. Each pole was joined to the base by a wooden screw. One of these had sheared off and needed to be replaced.

MATERIALS AND EQUIPMENT

- PVA (white) glue
- snap clamp
- flat-bladed knife
- brass pins (tacks)
- hammer
- pliers
- softwood
- band saw
- moulding plane
- sash clamp
- pincers
- utility knife
- chisel
- masking tape
- G-clamps

SECURING AND REPLACING VENEER

Securing loose veneer is a straightforward procedure, but replacing veneer is a more complicated process, mainly because care needs to be taken to find a good match. To secure the veneer to a curved area, a piece of softwood will need to be cut and shaped to fit the curve, in the same way as a counter-core was cut on p.75. This shaped piece is known as a jig.

1 Place the base section on a workbench. Apply PVA (white) glue to any cracks and insert slivers of wood if they are wide. Apply a snap clamp and leave to dry.

2 Reattach the loose veneer by pulling it up gently and applying PVA glue to the core using a flat-bladed knife.

3 Tap in two or three small brass pins (tacks) to hold the veneer in place, then snip off the ends with pliers, leaving enough showing to allow their removal with pincers later.

4 Prepare a jig to fit the concave area. Place newspaper between the jig and the veneer to prevent any excess glue bonding them together. Secure with a sash clamp and leave to dry for a few hours, then remove the clamp and jig. Pull out the pins with pincers.

5 Replace the missing end pieces of veneer first, as these must be laid over the top edge. Cut the replacement veneer to size with a utility knife and apply PVA glue to the core. Place the veneer on the glue, use the sash clamp and jig to secure it, and leave to dry.

6 Lay the replacement veneer for the top of the base over the damaged area. Ascertain how much of the old veneer will have to be removed in order to provide a straight line for the new piece to butt up to (meet). Cut along this line with a utility knife. ▷

Securing and replacing veneer...continued

7 Remove the splintered edge of the old veneer by sliding a sharp chisel between the veneer and the core. Tape the new veneer in place and turn the base over.

8 Mark the shape of the concave base on the new veneer with a pencil. Turn the base back over, remove the veneer and cut along the pencil line with a utility knife.

9 Glue the veneer in position and tap in two or three brass pins. Snip off their ends, apply G-clamps and glue blocks, and leave to dry. Remove the clamps and the pins. Repeat this process for all loose and missing veneer.

REPAIRING THE FEET AND THE POLE

The carved knurl feet are made up from two pieces of wood, which was typical of this type of foot construction. The top section has become detached and lost, and so a new scrolling top part must be carved. The feet are made from rosewood, but walnut, if stained, makes a suitable substitute. The pole needs a new screw thread to attach it to the base, and this must be turned using a box of a suitable size.

MATERIALS AND EQUIPMENT

• well-figured walnut	• fine brush
	• rubber
• PVA (white) or animal glue	• well-seasoned beech
• carving tools	• large gouge
• fine-grade sandpaper	• callipers
• screwdriver	• chisel
• fine wire (steel) wool	• box
	• soft cloth (cotton rag)
• polish	• wax

1 The knurl feet comprise two sections. The first is the actual foot that rests on the ground and the second is the rolling scroll at the top. A number of these scrolls are missing from the feet.

▷ **3** Sketch out the shape of the missing scroll, then, using the appropriate carving tools, shape and carve it to match a scroll on another foot. When it is finished, clean it up using fine-grade sandpaper. Repeat this process for the other damaged feet.

2 The knurl feet, like the pole screen, are made from rosewood, but since rosewood is difficult to source, a suitable piece of well-figured walnut has been chosen instead. Glue the walnut block to the damaged foot.

4 Screw the repaired feet temporarily in position on the newly restored base to make sure that everything fits correctly prior to being glued.

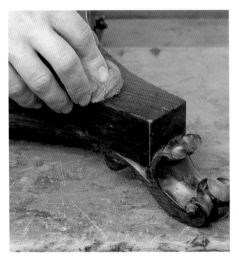

5 ◁ Remove the loose surface dirt and wax using fine wire (steel) wool prior to polishing. This will enable the fresh polish to bind to the exisiting finish.

6 ▷ The repaired feet can now be removed again to aid the process of polishing. Apply polish to the surface using a fine brush. Charge a rubber with further polish and apply to the feet to give an even finish all over (see pp.60–61).

Screw threads

The construction method used to attach the pole to the base is a screw thread. On one of the pole screens this has broken and so a new one must be turned and then cut using a box cutter (see below). Hard beech is the best wood to use as it will be both strong enough for the repair and hard enough to maintain a good edge on the thread.

7 Turn a new screw thread for the pole (see box left) out of well-seasoned beech, then fit the pole to the base. Charge a rubber with polish and apply a layer to the pole. Cut back the finish with wax to complete the work (see p.61).

Above: *The finished, polished and restored pole screen base.*   ▷

Making a frame

The new oval frame is constructed on a template (pattern) made from MDF (medium-density fiberboard). This template is used for both the frame and rim, which is made of strips of veneer and pieces of cross-grain rosewood. A tailor-made band clamp, fashioned from a steel tape, is used to secure the several thin layers of veneer that make up the rim. The moulded front of the frame is constructed from numerous pieces of solid rosewood, meticulously shaped and then attached to the rim. So that the frame has the same patina and colour as the base of the pole screen, the same rosewood veneer was used for the base and the outside of the frame. However, walnut veneer, which is cheaper than rosewood, could be used for the inner parts of the laminate.

MATERIALS AND EQUIPMENT

- plywood
- jigsaw (saber saw)
- fabric
- MDF (medium-density fiberboard)
- steel straightedge
- dividers
- hammer
- oval nails
- string
- pincers
- band saw
- steel band
- centre punch
- drill
- metal drill bit
- countersunk drill bit
- hardwood blocks
- screws
- screwdriver
- file
- clamp
- veneer for core
- facing plane
- depth gauge
- utility knife
- block plane
- masking tape
- large board
- newspaper
- brush
- PVA (white) glue
- small pieces of wood
- rosewood veneer
- scotch glue
- sponge
- cabinet scraper

MAKING THE RIM

The moulded front of the frame will be attached to the rim, while the glass, fabric and backing board will sit within it, so it needs to be both strong and regular in shape. It is made by layering veneer around a template, fixing it with glue and clamping it with a band clamp made specially for this project.

1 Prior to making the new frame, ascertain the correct diameter of the oval to suit the chosen fabric. To do this, cut a plywood oval with a jigsaw (saber saw) and place it over the material. This avoids the costly mistake of making a frame that is too small.

2 Cut a piece of MDF (medium-density fiberboard) with a jigsaw to a size just bigger than the frame, and place it on the bench. Draw two lines bisecting the MDF into quarters using a steel straightedge.

◁ **3** Divide the height and width of the oval frame in half. Mark each half-length on corresponding arms of the cross by scribing them with dividers.

▷ **4** Set the dividers to half the length of the oval. Place one point of the dividers on the mark indicating the width of the oval and scribe a line through one length line. Repeat this along the other length line.

5 Hammer an oval nail into each of the scribed marks on the length line and the outer mark on the width line. Tie string around the nails, allowing no slackness. Remove the nail from the width line.

6 Hold a sharp pencil inside the string and draw around the two nails, keeping tension on the string at all times.

7 Cut along the line with a band saw. The resulting oval shape will match the chosen size of the frame and will be used as the template (pattern) for making the frame.

8 Make a band clamp following the instructions on p.17. Band clamps have to be tailored to the rim they are going to fit, and therefore they must be custom made for the job and cannot be bought.

9 Select enough sheets of the cheaper veneer that is being used for the core to make five or six layers around the edge of the template. Place the veneer on the workbench and rough the surface with a facing plane.

10 Set a depth gauge to slightly wider than the template edge. Place the veneer on a flat surface and run the gauge along it. Use a utility knife to cut the veneer, along the gauge marks to a length slightly longer than the template rim.

11 Score and cut five more strips of veneer. Taper one end of two of the lengths of veneer with a block plane. These will be the first and last lengths to go around the rim, and paring them down prevents a step from forming on the rim.

12 Cover the edge of the template with masking tape and screw it to a large board covered with newspaper. Tape one of the planed-end strips of veneer to the template, wrap the veneer around the template and mark where it overlaps the secured end.

13 Remove the veneer strip from the template and brush PVA (white) glue on to the underside of the overlapping section only. Wrap the veneer strip around the template again and press it firmly to stick the overlapping ends together. ▷

Making the rim...continued

14 Add the remaining strips of veneer, applying glue to the previous layer before butting up the next strip. Use masking tape to secure the end of one strip to the start of the next. Finish with the planed-end strip.

15 Apply the band clamp and clamp the hardwood blocks to create the tension. Leave to dry for at least 12 hours, then remove the band clamp.

16 Raise the rim clear of the template, resting it on small pieces of wood, then use a block plane to smooth the rim edge. Turn the rim over, and plane the underside. Remove the rim and unscrew the template.

17 Cut a strip of rosewood veneer to the same height as the rim and long enough to go around the rim once exactly. Cut the ends square. Coat the inner surface of the strip thoroughly with scotch glue.

18 Place the veneer on the rim, joining the ends exactly. Place the rim on the template, secure it in a vice and use the back of a hammer to press the veneer into place. Dip the hammer into hot water to stop it sticking.

19 Leave the veneer to dry in the vice then lightly clean up the surface of the outer veneer with a cabinet scraper. Remove the rim from the template, which will be used for making the frame moulding.

MAKING THE FRAME MOULDING

The moulded front of the frame is made from rosewood that matches the rosewood veneer. Pieces of cross-grain wood need to be cut to fit the rim, then planed into shape.

MATERIALS AND EQUIPMENT

- rosewood
- dividers
- band saw
- rim template
- utility knife
- jigsaw (saber saw)
- masking tape
- chisel
- PVA (white) glue

- G-clamps
- spokeshave
- depth gauge
- snap clamp
- drill
- fine-grade sandpaper
- cork block
- flat-bladed knife
- hammer

- roughing plane blade
- scotch glue
- sealer
- rubber
- shellac polish
- clear beeswax
- soft cloth (cotton rag)
- glass

- plywood
- coloured silk
- small screws
- screwdriver
- brass brackets
- laminated walnut strip
- black water stain
- steel panel pins (tacks)

1 Cut the rosewood into small sections of the desired thickness. Use a pair of dividers to mark the approximate width of the frame, allowing extra for shaping (see step 8). Cut the rosewood into the required cross-grain size with a band saw.

2 Place the rosewood underneath the template, with the area left for shaping protruding. Score the rosewood around the template curve with a utility knife. Cut this line with a band saw.

3 After each piece is cut, hold it next to the preceding piece and make a pencil line to provide a smooth joint.

4 Cut along the pencil line with a sharp chisel to make sure that the ends of the pieces butt up (meet) exactly. Tape the new piece in place. Repeat this process until the entire frame is complete.

5 The frame is now ready to be glued. Make sure that there are no gaps between the rosewood pieces at this stage.

6 Cut some newspaper to the same size as the rosewood pieces and glue a piece to the underside of one of the wood sections with PVA (white) glue, to stop the frame sticking to the template. Apply glue to the edges of the wood, and a small amount to the paper.

7 Flap back the other pieces out of the way, then place the first piece of rosewood in position on the template and secure it with a G-clamp. Follow this method for the remaining pieces of rosewood, gluing the joints together at their edges. Leave to dry.

8 Remove the clamps, put the template and frame in a vice, and plane the outer edge with a spokeshave. Out of the vice, set a depth gauge to the frame width and score a line around the inner edge of the frame.

9 Clamp the template to the workbench so that part of it overhangs the edge. Drill a pilot hole in the template, against the inner edge of the frame, then use a jigsaw to cut around the scored line in sections.

10 Put the frame, still attached to the MDF, back in the vice and clean up the inner edge with a spokeshave until the surface is completely smooth and flush with the scored line.

▷

Making the frame moulding...continued

11 Clamp the frame and MDF layer to the workbench. Use the spokeshave to mould a convex shape on the front of the frame.

12 Remove the frame and MDF from the clamp. Continue shaping the frame by sanding it with fine-grade sandpaper wrapped around a cork block. The frame must be smooth and even.

13 Place the frame and MDF on a level surface and insert a flat-bladed knife between the two pieces. Lightly tap the edge of the blade with a hammer until the frame comes away, probably in pieces.

14 Place the pieces of frame in the correct order on the flat surface. Use a blade from a roughing plane to remove any remaining traces of glue or newspaper from the underside of the rosewood.

15 Apply scotch glue to the underside of the outer half of each frame section, and place the pieces on the rim, making sure that each piece goes back into the same position it was in on the template. Leave to dry.

16 When the rim is dry, sand it with fine-grade sandpaper and apply some sealer with a brush. This seals the grain before it is polished. Charge a rubber with polish and apply layers to the frame (see pp.60–61).

17 Give the finished frame a layer of wax to cut back the shine (see p.61). It should now match the base of the pole screen in colour, grain and finish.

18 Cut a piece of glass (or take it to a glazier) and a piece of 3mm (⅛in) thick plywood to fit inside the rim, and another small piece of plywood for the bracket mounting plate.

19 Cover the plywood back board and the bracket mounting plate with a suitable coloured silk and join them by screwing them together from the inside.

20 Screw either the original or suitable replacement brackets into place. Make sure that they are in the correct position on the back and not upside down. Fit the glass, the piece of fabric and the back board.

21 The back is held in place by a laminated walnut strip. Shape this by feeding it into hot water until it is pliable. Use the reservoir pot from the scotch glue for this process.

22 When it is wet and pliable, the walnut strip has shaped itself and is suitable to be fitted on to the inside of the rim. Leave it to dry naturally.

23 Fit the walnut strip, now shaped into a curve, inside the frame, trimming it to size with a utility knife. Remove it and apply a black water stain to match the rim (see p.63).

24 Tap the walnut strip back into place , and fix it with steel panel pins (tacks). Attach the frame to the stand using the brass brackets. Repeat for the other screen.

Above: *A pair of rosewood pole screens, sympathetically restored to their original condition.*

GLOSSARY

animal glue Also known as scotch glue and traditionally used from the 17th century onwards.

astragals Glazing bars on cabinet furniture, forming a geometric pattern.

bain-marie A pot containing hot water in which another container, holding animal glue, gesso or bole, for example, can be gently heated.

banding Decorative inlays of veneer that are used for aesthetic effect. They can be either long-grained or cross-grained and on earlier pieces can be joined to give a chevron effect, known as herringbone.

blister A bubble that forms on a surface when part of the veneer has become detached from its core.

blooming The name given to the white marks left on a polished surface that has been water-damaged or chilled.

bole A clay-like substance that is used in the gilding process.

boulle Also known as buhl, this is the use of fine brass inlay inset into tortoiseshell or ebony backgrounds.

bracket foot A square foot which might have a shaped profile on the inside. The foot most commonly used during the 18th century.

breaker A piece or a collection of pieces of furniture used in the restoration of another item of furniture.

bun feet A ball type of foot favoured during the 17th century and replaced by the bracket foot in the 18th century.

butterfly key A butterfly-shaped piece of wood used to secure and hold splits. It is inset into a piece so that the grain runs at right angles to the main wood. Also known as a dovetail key.

carcass The actual framework of a piece of furniture. Depending on the period, this would be either in the solid or veneered.

cascamite A glue used when forming laminates or shape work. It is very strong but also brittle.

cock beading Thin strips of decorative beading often found around drawer fronts.

colour The tone or shade that wood develops over time.

conservation To maintain a piece by undertaking as little work as possible so as not to alter its present or original form (*see* restoration).

core The moulded shape on to which veneer or mouldings are applied.

cornice The top of a carcass piece of furniture often decorated with dental mouldings, cross bandings or a pediment.

cross-grain mouldings Wood applied to a softwood backing and planed to a moulded profile, applied to a carcass for aesthetic reasons. Introduced during the 17th century, they are more decorative than long-grain mouldings.

Cuban mahogany Mahogany imported from Cuba during the 18th and 19th centuries and the preferred wood for quality furniture. It is densely grained and red in tone when first polished.

cutting gauge A tool fitted with a small blade that is used across the grain to cut a groove. Often used prior to fitting boxwood lines.

de-nibbing The removal of dust that has combined with polish to form small raised nibs on a surface after polishing. This is done by lightly using fine wire wool in the direction of the grain. The surface is then waxed.

dental mouldings Small rectangular pieces applied to a cornice and resembling square teeth. Popular during the mid-18th century.

dovetail saw A fine-bladed saw used for cutting accurate and delicate dovetails.

escutcheon The brassware used in conjunction with locks for both aesthetic and protective reasons.

fading/fad Filling the grain in wood with a mixture of polish and pumice powder. The cloth with which it is applied is known as a fad.

fire gilding A mixture of gold and mercury applied to a metal base and heated until the mercury evaporates and binds the gold to the metal. Favoured during the 18th century; used on the mounts and handles of the finest pieces.

French curve A kidney-shaped scraper used on concave curves.

French polishing Using shellac polish, which is usually applied with a linen and wadding (batting) rubber.

fret A lattice-like decoration, in which open fret is pierced and blind fret is applied to a solid background.

gauge sticks Two lengths of stick which are held together and used to check the equal diagonal measure of a frame to ensure it is square.

gesso A plaster-like substance that is used in the gilding process.

graining Using surface stains and colours to mimic the grain of a solid piece of wood. Favoured during the early 19th century.

Honduras mahogany Mahogany imported from Honduras during the 18th and 19th centuries and favoured for carcass construction.

kickers Strips of wood applied to the inside carcass of a chest, running along the top of the drawer linings, to stop the drawers tipping forward when extended.

linings The name given to the sides and often the bottom of a drawer.

long-grain mouldings Mouldings planed from one length of wood along the grain and applied to a carcass for aesthetic or structural reasons.

marquetry Inlays of decorative scenes.

marriage Two parts of a piece of furniture that started life separately but have now been brought together. Such an example would be a bureau bookcase in which both halves would have started life with another part.

mortise The hollow housing part of a mortise and tenon joint, which is the most widely used joint in furniture construction.

mortise gauge A marking tool that has a small steel point and is used along the grain to mark the shoulders of a mortise.

overloe A shaped block used in conjunction with sandpaper.

parquetry Inlays of geometric patterns.

patera A round or oval, raised decoration often found on cornices or the tops of legs. Can also be used in veneer form.

patination This refers to the build up of waxes, natural greases and dust that over numerous years combines to form a desirable finish on a surface.

pediment Found on top of a carcass and, depending on the period, can be arched, broken-arched or swan-necked in shape.

piecrust The name used to describe the shape of a top usually applying to a tripod table. The top, as the name suggests, looks like the top of a pinched pastry pie top.

plinth The platform base on which a carcass will sit.

PVA glue Polyvinylacetate glue, also known as white glue. Ideal for day to day use.

reeded decoration A raised decoration of parallel, tapering lines, usually found on chair and table legs.

reeds Raised dome-shaped decoration applied along the length of a surface.

restoration To undertaken any necessary work to return a piece as near as possible to its original form but retaining its integrity (*see* conservation).

revive a surface The action of attending to any minor damage or surface oxidation of a polished surface while not repolishing the whole top.

rubber Wadding (batting) wrapped in linen, which is used to apply shellac polish.

runners The strips of wood attached to the bottom or sides of a drawer on which the drawer will run. Sometimes also found as part of the carcass.

scratch box A workshop-made tool that allows parallel reeds to be scratched on a leg (*see* reeded decoration).

shellac Polish that is obtained from the shellac beetle.

skiver Leather taken from sheep. Not as good quality as cow hide.

splay feet A shaped bracket foot that is splayed in profile. Favoured during the late 18th century.

spring clip A workshop-made cramping device made from upholstery springs. Ideal for securing awkward shapes.

stains Usually bought in powder form and mixed with water, spirit or oil depending on the intended use.

stringing Thin lines of inlay, usually of ebony or box, which were used for both aesthetic reasons and as protective edges.

tenon The protruding part of a mortise and tenon joint, which is the most widely used joint in furniture construction.

twist When wood bows in two directions.

warp When a piece of wood has bowed along its length or width.

FURTHER INFORMATION

British Antique Furniture
Restorers' Association (BAFRA)
The Old Rectory
Warmwell, Dorchester
Dorset DT2 8HQ
UK
Tel/fax: 01305 854822
Email: headoffice@bafra.org.uk
Web: www.bafra.org.uk

British Antique Dealers'
Association (BADA)
20 Rutland Gate
London SW7 1BD
UK
Tel: 020 7589 4128
Fax: 020 7581 9083
Web: www.bada.org

Association of Art and Antique
Dealers' (LAPADA)
535 Kings Road
Chelsea
London SW10 0SZ
UK
Tel: 020 7823 3511
Fax: 020 7823 3522
Web: www.lapada.co.uk

Association of Restorers
8 Medford Place
New Hartford
NY 13413
USA
Tel: (315) 733–1952
Fax: (315) 724–7231
Web: www.assoc-restorers.com

Art and Antique Dealers' League of
America, Inc. (AADLA)
1040 Madison Avenue
New York
NY 10021
USA
Tel: (212) 879–7558
Fax: (212) 772–7197
www.artantiquedealersleague.com

The National Antique & Art
Dealers Association of America, Inc.
220 East 57th Street
New York
NY 10022
USA
Tel: (212) 826–9707
Fax: (212) 832–9493

Australian Antique Dealers'
Association
PO Box 24
Malvern
Victoria 3144
Australia
Tel: (03) 9576 2275
Fax: (03) 9576 2106
Email: secaada@ozemail.com.au

PICTURE CREDITS

INDEX

W.J. COOK & SONS

W.J.Cook & Sons was established by Bill Cook in 1962. His reputation for outstanding work quickly spread and since those early days clients have included the British Royal Household and Government, museums, leading collectors, dealers and private individuals. While still retaining a London workshop, the business is based in Marlborough, Wiltshire. With the cabinet-making, machine and polishing shops it is a business that is recognized as one of the leaders in its field. After training at the London College of Furniture, three of Bill's sons joined the business and have helped develop and further expand its range and facilities. Now their own children are being encouraged to pick up the tools with a view to taking the family tradition to a third generation.

The services carried out are many and include cabinet-making, gilding, carving, polishing, lock repairs, leathering and upholstery. Being a true family business it means that every restoration commission is undertaken with great care. With over 40 years of experience at the very highest level, together with an extensive in-house

Left: *from left to right, Bill, Stephen, Richard, Billy and (seated) Catherine Cook.*

library and access to furniture archives, any restoration carried out is authentic in every detail.

Virtually all the restoration work is still carried out using 18th- and 19th-century tools: their band saw was used in the construction of the panelling for the *Queen Mary*.

A final note: antique furniture if badly restored can rarely be returned to its original glory. Therefore, it is important that a suitably qualified restorer should be consulted when necessary.

High Trees House
Savernake Forest
Marlborough
Wiltshire
SN8 4NE
01672 513017
william.cook@virgin.net
www.wjcookandsons.com

167 Battersea High Street
London
SW11 3JS
020 7736 5329

Author's acknowledgements

When approached to write this book we were delighted to accept. For a number of years we have been acutely aware of the absence of any book that was written and extensively photographed in a commercial restoration workshop and which showed and explained clearly how various techniques are carried out on a day to day basis. Drawing from over 40 years of experience and a lifetime's collection of materials and tools, we hope to have given the reader an authoritative insight into the subject.

While the overwhelming majority of work was undertaken "in house", there are grateful thanks due to others who have been invaluable in their help both with advice and in the use of their facilities: Barry Ansell of R.D. Robins Ltd, London, on upholstery; Geoff Collier of Colliers Castings, Hooe, on casting methods; Les Crispin of Capital Crispin Veneer, London, on veneers, Alan Dallison on leathers, Bob Dunn of A. Dunn & Son, Chelmsford, on marquetry; and Optimum Brasses, Tiverton, on brassware.

Special thanks go to the staff in our workshops for making sure that the work needed for this book was always ready on time. A big thank you goes to Paul Lyon for his sterling work, without which this book would have been impossible.

On a personal note, like all family businesses, an unsung hero is our mother Catherine who has always been there keeping the wheels turning. Thanks also to my brothers Richard and Stephen with whom it is very much a team effort, and not to forget Justin, who has chosen to follow his own path.

Thanks to all those who have been encouraging and supportive throughout the whole process of writing this book, including Richard my life-long friend, for his humour, often dispensed from across the world, Nathalie, whose words of wisdom, while not always fully appreciated are always carefully considered, and my three sons William, Henry and James, for just being themselves.

Finally this book is for my father from his sons, and for our sons and daughters from their fathers in the hope that they may one day take the business onwards for another generation.

BILLY COOK